The Shī'a Imams
in the words of
Preeminent Sunni Scholarship

A New Case for the Rightfulness of the
Claim to Leadership of the Twelve Shī'a Imams

Masoud Emami

Translated and Annotated by
Blake Archer Williams

Copyright © 2021 by Blake Archer Williams

All rights reserved. No part of this publication may be reproduced, distributed, or transmitted in any form or by any means, including photocopying, recording, or other electronic or mechanical methods, without the prior written permission of the publisher, except in the case of brief quotations embodied in critical reviews and certain other noncommercial uses permitted by copyright law. For permission requests, write to the publisher, addressed "Attention: - Permissions (Shia Imams in Summi scholarship)," at the email address below.

Lantern Publications
info@lanternpublications.com
www.lanternpublications.com

Ordering Information:
Quantity sales. Special discounts are available on quantity purchases by corporations, associations, and others. For details, contact the distributor at the address below.

Shia Books Australia
www.shiabooks.com.au
info@shiabooks.com.au

ISBN: 978-1-922583-07-9

First Edition
Cover: 'The Scholars' – Painting by Austrian master Ludwig Deutsch (1901). (Public Domain)

In the Name of God,

the Most Compassionate, the Most Merciful

Prayers of God's Peace and Blessings

In keeping with the Islamic practice of showing respect for the name of God, and sending prayers of God's peace and blessings whenever the name of His blessed Prophet, Lady Fātema, and the Twelve Imams is mentioned, as well as for asking God to hasten the reappearance of the Lord of the Age on the Earthly plane, one or more of the following Arabic symbols have been employed throughout the text. They are repeated for their great rewards.

 Used exclusively after the name of God, meaning "the Sublimely Exalted", or, as a prayer, "[May His name be] Sublimely Exalted".

 Used exclusively after the name of the Prophet, meaning "May the peace and blessings of God be unto him and unto [the purified and inerrant members of] his family"

 Used for any of the Twelve Imams or past prophets of God , meaning "May God's peace be unto him".

 Used for two or more of the Twelve Imams or past prophets of God, meaning "May God's peace be unto them".

 Used for Lady Fātema, meaning "May God's peace be unto her".

 Used for a plurality of the Fourteen Immaculates, meaning "May God's peace be unto them all collectively".

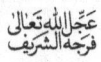 Used for the Lord of the Age (the Twelfth Imam), meaning "May God hasten the advent of his noble person".

A Note on Transliteration

The Persian words and Persian words of Arabic origin referred to in this book have been transliterated as they are pronounced (as opposed to all standard academic transliteration systems that transliterate words as they are written). As such, there is no 'system' of transliteration, such as that used by the Library of Congress, because pronunciations vary from region to region. Nevertheless, the reason this approach was preferred is that while it is necessarily somewhat subjective, it has an advantage that of actually representing the sounds of the words as they are meant to be pronounced. This might not be a factor among a group of orientalist scholars who already know how the words are pronounced and will pronounce the words correctly, despite their transliteration; but the intelligent general reader who is the target audience of this book is not in a position to be able to differentiate between the 'solar' (*shamsi*) and 'lunar' (*qamari*) letters of the Arabic alphabet, and thus, unlike the orientalist scholar, will mispronounce an-Najaf as al-Najaf. The matter becomes even more complicated when it comes to the name of the august daughter of the Most Noble Prophet ﷺ, Lady Fātemat oz-Zahrā ﷺ, the correct pronunciation of whose name is an essential consideration for the Shī'a faithful. It is the preclusion of these kinds of pronunciation errors that have motivated us to use the 'as pronounced' as opposed to the 'as written' approach.

That having been said, there are several Arabic words whose transliteration based on the as-written system(s) has become so prevalent that seeing a transliteration other than what has unfortunately become the standard fare would seem awkward and out of place. To preclude this, we have chosen to use what has become standard in such cases. Instances of these cases include the words Quran (rather than Qoran or Koran), Muslim (rather than Moslem), and Muhammad (rather than Mohammad ﷺ, using the letter 'o' to designate the *dhamma* over the *mīm*, this being the correct English equivalent symbol for the phoneme that is symbolized by the *dhamma*).

Contents

INTRODUCTION 1

EPISTEMOLOGICAL FOUNDATIONS 3

    1. Criteria of Action in the Event of Doubt 4

    2. Historical Precedence of Evidentialism 10

    3. Evidentialism in Practice 14

THE APPLICATION OF EVIDENTIALISM IN PROOFS OF THE IMĀMATE 17

    1: Twelve Princes from the Progeny of Ishmael 18

    2: Twelve Successors (khalīfa) after the Prophet 20

    3: Twelve Great Personages in One Uninterrupted Chain 23

THE EVIDENCE 37

    1. Imam Ali b. Abī-Tāleb 37

    2. Imam Hasan b. Ali 59

    3. Imam Hosayn b. Ali 62

    4. Imam Ali b. Hosayn Zeyn ol-Ābedīn 69

    5. Imam Muhammad b. Ali al-Bāqer 80

    6. Imam Ja'far b. Muhammad as-Sādeq 85

    7. Imam Mūsā b. Ja'far al-Kāzem 101

    8. Imam Ali b. Mūsā ar-Reḍā 107

    9. Imam Muhammad b. Ali al-Jawād 111

    10. Imam Hasan b. Ali al-Hādī 114

    11. Imam Hasan b. Muhammad al-Askarī 115

CONCLUDING REMARKS 117

BIBLIOGRAPHY 122

ENDNOTES 124

The Shī'a Imāms in the Words of Sunni Scholarship

Introduction

This book is a presentation of the views of a large representative sample of the opinion of Sunni scholarship on the exalted rank of eleven Imams of the Shīʿa in terms of their breadth of knowledge and spiritual station. This overall representative view is then used as the basis for the proof of the rightfulness of their claim to leadership of the community. This proof is based on specific rational epistemological principles which we shall explore briefly in the first chapter of the book. Based on these proffered epistemological principles, the nature of the probative force of this proof is such that it is capable of being strengthened with the addition of other supplementary evidence and factors. We therefore bring to bear some of these factors as evidence in another section of the book. The application of the rationale provided by this supplementary evidence has been used extensively in the past and has a long history in the annals of apologetics and dogmatic argumentation (*kalām*), but the primary proof here presented has not, to the best of my knowledge, been used before in the history of demonstrations which relate to the doctrine of the imāmate. Thus, it can be said that what is presented in this essay is a new proof for [the rightfulness of the claim to] the imāmate of the Twelve Imams of the Shīʿa (unto all of whom be God ❧ peace).

1 Epistemological Foundations

The epistemological assumption of the proof presented in this essay is that evidential proofs are valid. Evidential proofs are proofs within a class of proofs which have their basis in the cumulative effect of the evidence and indications at hand have on informed and well-considered scholarly opinion. This proof brings about a preponderance in the probability or likelihood of the veracity of a given proposed option, among other possibilities. According to this view, which can be called "evidentialism,"[1] valid arguments are not restricted to those which are premised on assumptions that are derived from the (limited and limiting) field of pure logic (which yield conclusions with absolute certainty[2]). On the contrary, evidentialism holds that the conclusions drawn from valid arguments by way of the cumulative effect just described (i.e. from less than proof positive premises, as opposed to the proof positive premises available in the domain of pure logic) are also capable of yielding conclusions in which one can, in good conscience, be certain. Furthermore, in order to establish a given hypothesis under the aegis of this epistemological rubric, every proffered proposition does not need to yield conclusions with absolute certainty by themselves; rather, it is possible to gather individual propositions, each of which does not in itself yield certainty, and to posit an argument where the cumulative effect of the totality of the various individual propositions or arguments brought to bear brings about a preponderance of opinion in favor of the argument being made, thereby ultimately yielding a conclusion the veracity of which one can be assured in good conscience.

People use evidentialism in their everyday lives in order to arrive at truth to the point that it is a norm, be this in the personal, social and even scientific spheres. A contemporary scholar has utilized a methodology which is based on something very close to evidentialism as a method for proving his religious beliefs.[3]

Finally, for putting an end to indecision for practical purposes (as opposed to principles of belief, for example), the ascendancy of the strongest possibility suffices for preferring one choice over other possibilities, and there is no need to arrive at a conclusion whose veracity is inwardly certain. Reason dictates that a person who must choose one of several options which are before him, who is unable to decide in favor of any of the possibilities in which he can be certain, must necessarily act upon the possibility which he deems to be the preponderant or the most likely option which will achieve his or her objective. The preference made in favor of a given possibility over the other available possibilities does not depend solely on the percentage of its likelihood but also depends on the probable value of the possibility as well as the cost of acting on that possibility. This point is in need of further explanation, which will be provided in the next section.

1. Criteria of Action in the Event of Doubt

In determining their objectives and ways of reaching those objectives, human beings look for certainty; but certainty is elusive, and what usually happens is that one takes strides in one direction or another upon which he has decided without having attained certainty as to whether the path he has chosen is the right one, and which only provides a possibility of arriving at his goal. Ignorance of future events and the unpredictability of events, such as the time of one's death, does not preclude man from taking action. This is because the ambiguities and uncertainties he faces in attaining to his objectives are so numerous in the physical and metaphysical realms that he is left with no choice other than to plan his life around these uncertainties as best he can.

In response to this basic human need, i.e. the need to make a decision as to what path to take among the many that are arrayed before him, the mind analyzes and triangulates, and, in short, carries out a series of specific calculations. Most of this logical processing is carried out at such speed that the subject is not even aware of its various phases at a conscious level. However, notwithstanding this, the subject arrives at the rational outcome of having chosen between one of the likely options (and avoiding the irrational outcome of having chosen the other less likely ones) by way of this logical process.

In analyzing this performance, we can conclude that the mind takes three criteria into consideration in its calculus of determining the preferable and rational option among the various choices before it. These are the following:

1. The likelihood of the various possibilities (or the likely percentage or "odds" of the various possibilities);
2. The probable value of the possibility; and finally,
3. The cost of acting on that possibility.

In other words, when confronted with a series of possibilities from which one must choose a single option (when he doubts his ultimate choice or cannot attain to certainty in it), one weighs the percentage of probability of each choice being the right one and chooses the most likely possibility. In addition to this, he also takes into account and factors in the significance and value of each possibility, giving preference to the more important one or the possibility with the greater value (however defined) in preference to ones which are less important/ significant or less valuable. Finally, the amount of effort and energy that must be expended in the execution of each option is also considered. The options with the smallest cost profiles are prioritized over those with greater impacts in terms of their execution cost.

None of these three criteria are determinative of the best option in themselves; rather, it is usually a process which takes into account the combined weighting of all three factors which causes one option to prevail over the rest. Of course, rare instances also might occur where one cannot arrive at a preferred option even after taking all three of these factors into account. In this event, man's reason tells him that he is free to choose any one of the various options which are equally weighted and preferred.

Thus, when confronted with a choice between several options, a rational person will seek to see the percentage of each option's probability of arriving at his desired goal. However, this is not the only factor he uses; the value of the objective which this probability-weighted path leads to is also factored into his calculus. It is certainly possible that the value of the objective or goal which a given path leads to becomes a reason for someone's choice of that option, even though the probability of its fruition is less than the other options he has. Similarly, together with these two factors, the execution costs are also factored into the calculus of any rational approach to making choices under conditions of uncertainty. Consequently, someone can abandon a choice that has a high percentage of probability of attaining to fruition and whose objective is highly valued based on its execution cost, which in this case would be deemed prohibitive. Thus, in conditions where certainty cannot be attained, it is a combination of all three of these factors, each of which is evaluated and weighted according to the prevalent conditions and the capacities of each individual, which ultimately reveals the best possible option.

Let us now clarify the matter of the evaluation of these factors by way of example. Imagine that a person is ambivalent about what subject he should study at university and has not as yet reached a decision. At the same time, he is determined to begin his studies, and he cannot delay his decision any longer. In this case, he will perforce take the aforementioned three factors into account in choosing his primary subject. First, he will calculate the probable percentage of his being accepted into each of the fields of study between which he is undecided. Needless to say, the subject which offers the highest likelihood of acceptance will be given preference. In addition to this consideration, the student's personal preference for the various subjects offered will be factored in, with the preferred subject being given preference over the others. Again, It is possible that he may have a lower likelihood of being accepted into the program that offers his preffered subject, however he would still give this program (subject) a higher preference than those he is more likely to be accepted into. At the same time as taking these two factors into account, our student will also factor in the third criterion, which is the amount of effort he will need to expend in order to matriculate and/ or graduate from a given program. Clearly, this factor plays a determinative role in the choice of a given field of study over other fields. Ultimately, the best option is decided upon after having gone through a process in which all three factors are considered and accounted for. Every rational human being grapples with these three factors in making the best decisions throughout his or her life from a field of probable alternative possibilities.

We humans probably go through this rational process each and every day of our lives, from trivial matters such as what to buy from what store, or the decision as to how best to get there and back, to broader considerations such as choosing one's spouse or career. It is a process that every rational person goes through when confronted with choices in which he cannot decide with absolute certainty (but only with degrees of certainty). There is no difference in its application when the ambiguity or lack of the ability to attain to certainty pertains to one's personal matters, family matters, social concerns or in matters of religious faith and belief. Therefore, an onus of responsibility falls on the shoulders of a rational person if an ambiguity exists in essential matters of faith, religious belief, or in the philosophical foundations of creedal matters, to engage rationally with the problem at hand and to analyze it using one's reason in order to arrive at the answer that resolves the ambiguity. If, in the course of ones analysis, one sees that one cannot attain certainty as to what the right answer is to a given question, and must perforce use an answer whose veracity is probabilistic at best as the basis of the action which he must take; he must then choose an option from the list of options all of which attain to some degree of doubt rather than to 100% certainty, and he must arrive at his preference by applying the process discussed above which takes into account a combination of the three factors of (1) the probability of success or fruition, (2) the value of the objective which can be attained by the option under consideration, and (3) the execution cost of each option. Therefore, a person who applies this process in the case of ambiguity or doubt concerning a decision of belief – irrespective of what ends he ultimately attains to – has taken the correct path and the rational path, and cannot and should not be subject to moral disapprobation.

The evaluation of the tripartite factors and acting on them necessitates the investigation of the available information concerning each of the possible paths that are before the prospective decision-maker. A person decides upon the probability of each path reaching his or her desired goal by factoring in the data about his or her objectives and the various paths that exist that can reach it, and determines the value of the objective which can be attained by each option under consideration and the execution cost of each option using this same goal-oriented information. Thus, the person who is uncertain as to what decision to make, no matter how much they might lack certain information (hence, his or her uncertainty concerning the right decision), generally has some idea of the path that is most likely to lead to success in attaining their objective. It is usually the case that information does exist to base one's decision on, but this information is incomplete. However this same incomplete information becomes the seedbed for the tripartite decision process which is the preliminary step that must be taken before the decision to act is taken .

The decision-maker evaluates the information which is at hand and places the evidence and indicators in favor of or against the veracity or falsity of each option side by side and ultimately decides the quantum of probability of each option's path successfully leading to its objective. The decision-maker must utilize his or her incomplete information in the processes having to do with the determination of the best probable value and the least probable execution cost in a similar way. Thus, the information that is available to the undecided person plays a fundamental role in the determination of the best possible course of action on the basis of the rational process which entails the three factors, no matter how incomplete this information might be.

Taking the available relevant information and systematically ordering them, and seeing how each datum relates to the various probable paths of the various objectives at hand is the epistemological methodology called Evidentialism. Under the auspices of this methodology it is possible for the proper gathering and analysis of the available data to lead to a definitive and conclusive choice of one of the possible options; and it is possible that this definition and certainty does not obtain, in which case the compiled and analyzed knowledge-base will remain at the level of indicators which militate for or mitigate against different possibilities and probabilities, and where the probative force of all the various possible choices remains uncertain and probabilistic. In this event, we must necessarily turn to the calculus involving the tripartite factors.

2. Historical Precedence of Evidentialism

Since acting on the basis of the tripartite factors while in doubt about a decision to be made is in accordance with one's rational mind, which is in turn in harmony with one's primordial (*fetric*[4]) disposition, and because each rational human being falls back on this method in his day to day life when he is ambiguous about a choice that is before him or about the choice of the various beliefs which confront him, it stands to reason that the historical record for its precedence in the history of humanity goes as far back as history itself.

The Noble Quran refers to this rational approach. The Quran argues with its interlocutors in two *āyāt*[5] concerning their skepticism and doubt, and posits even the acceptance of the religion revealed by the Quran as a rational matter. In Surat al-Fūsilāt we see the following āya:

$$قُلْ أَرَأَيْتُمْ إِنْ كَانَ مِنْ عِنْدِ اللَّهِ ثُمَّ كَفَرْتُمْ بِهِ مَنْ أَضَلُّ مِمَّنْ هُوَ فِي شِقَاقٍ بَعِيدٍ$$

> [41:52] Have you given thought [to how you will fare] *if* this be truly [a revelation] from God ﷻ, the while you deny its truth? Who could be more astray than one who places himself [so] deeply in the wrong?

In this revelation, the word 'if' is used, which denotes cases where more than one possibility exists or can exist, i.e. when there is some uncertainty or doubt. The Quran speaks to its interlocutors on the assumption of their uncertainty and doubt concerning its own veracity. Emphasizing the likelihood and severity of damage to the souls of the interlocutors who defy its call, the Quran calls on them to attain to faith in its message.

And in āya 28 of the Sūraᵗ al-Ghāfer we see the following:

وَقَالَ رَجُلٌ مُّؤْمِنٌ مِّنْ آلِ فِرْعَوْنَ يَكْتُمُ إِيمَانَهُ أَتَقْتُلُونَ رَجُلًا أَن يَقُولَ رَبِّيَ اللَّهُ وَقَدْ جَاءَكُم بِالْبَيِّنَاتِ مِن رَّبِّكُمْ ۖ وَإِن يَكُ كَاذِبًا فَعَلَيْهِ كَذِبُهُ ۖ وَإِن يَكُ صَادِقًا يُصِبْكُم بَعْضُ الَّذِي يَعِدُكُمْ ۖ إِنَّ اللَّهَ لَا يَهْدِي مَنْ هُوَ مُسْرِفٌ كَذَّابٌ

[40:28] At that, a believing man of Pharaoh's family, who [until then] had concealed his faith, exclaimed: "Would you slay a man because he says, 'God 🕌 is my Lord of Providence - seeing, withal, that he has brought you all evidence of this truth from your Lord of Providence? Now *if* he be a liar, his lie will fall back on him; but if he is a man of truth, something [of the punishment] whereof he warns you is bound to befall you: for, verily, God 🕌 would not grace with His guidance one who has wasted his own self by lying [about Him].

The "believing man of Pharaoh's family" argues with his interlocutors assuming their uncertainty and doubt about the rightfulness of Moses, unto whom be God's 🕌 peace, and he too uses the conditional article 'if', and he too warns of dire consequences that will befall them if they slay a man because he says, 'God 🕌 is my Lord of Providence…'

The Noble Quran uses what we have called an Evidentialist methodology for proving the most important of religious teachings. The Noble Quran brings to our attention the evidence and indications that exist "[through what they perceive] in the utmost horizons [of the universe] and within themselves" [reference to the Quran 41:53] in order to demonstrate the reality of the oneness of God 🕌, prophethood, and the life of the hereafter, all three of which are the most important principles of faith in Islam. In other words, the Quran does not go about proving the principles of the Islamic faith by way of rational proofs which belong to the domain of pure logic and which yield absolute certainty; rather, it brings man's attention to the evidence and indications which, while each of them do not yield certainty individually, the cumulative effect of their probative force is such that it brings about a preponderance of opinion in favor of the argument being made. And it is possible for the level of the probability of the veracity of the religious teachings of the Quran to ascend to such a level in an ordinary person where he or she becomes psychologically and inwardly certain of the truth of these teachings. The Noble Quran usually refers to these evidences and indications as āyas (signs, indications) and as bayinna (clear evidence; proofs). The following noble āya provides clear evidence of the evidentialist method at work:

سَنُرِيهِمْ آيَاتِنَا فِي الْآفَاقِ وَفِي أَنْفُسِهِمْ حَتَّىٰ يَتَبَيَّنَ لَهُمْ أَنَّهُ الْحَقُّ ۗ أَوَلَمْ يَكْفِ بِرَبِّكَ أَنَّهُ عَلَىٰ كُلِّ شَيْءٍ شَهِيدٌ

[41:53] In time We shall make them fully understand Our messages [through what they perceive] in the utmost horizons [of the universe] and within themselves so that it will become clear unto them that this [revelation] is indeed the truth. [Still,] is it not enough [for them to know] that thy Lord of Providence is witness unto everything?[6]

The present indicative form of the verb *sanurīhim* in the opening phrase *In time We shall make them fully understand* denotes a continuity and is indicative of God ﷻ volition to show humanity His signs, is a continuous action which shall continue as long as he is capable of perceiving truth and attaining to certainty in it.

The use of this methodology can also be seen in the ḥadīth reports of the Ahl al-Bayt ﷺ (the Members of the Household of the Prophet ﷺ). In responding

1 Epistemological Foundations

to Eben Abī'l-'Owjā' who denied the existence of God 🕮 and the Domain of the Invisible (*ālam-e ghayb*: the metaphysical hypostasis; the underlying substantive domain that is beyond the ken of ordinary human perception) and considered the ritual conduct of the Hajj pilgrims to be contrary to human norms, Imam Sādeq (s) engages him in a discussion based on his denial of the world to come in the hereafter, pointing out the enormous benefits of following the teachings of the Quran in the event that these teachings are true, and the lack of any detriment in the event that they are false. Addressing Eben Abī'l-'Owjā', Imam Sādeq says:

> "If the truth is that which these pilgrims believe – and in my opinion, this is the case – then they will reach felicity in the hereafter and you will be in hardship; and if the truth is that which you assert – which in my opinion, this is not the case – then you and they will be equal [in your fates]."[7]

Similar words are found in a quatrain attributed to Imam Ali:

> Monjam and Tabīb both say that there shall be no [Day of] Resurrection, and that bodies will not be gathered. If the words of you two turns out to be right, I have not suffered any loss; but if my claim is correct, the loss will be yours.[8]

In another hadīth report of the Commander of the Faithful (Imam Ali), it is related that he said:

> If the truth is that which you believe, all will be delivered; but if it is as I see it, then you will be condemned and I will be delivered.

Blaize Pascal (1623-1662 of Clermont-Ferrand, France) was a French mathematician, physicist, inventor, and Christian philosopher. He demonstrated a proof which has become known as Pascal's Wager, in which he argued that "it is in one's own best interest to behave as if God ﷻ exists, since the possibility of eternal punishment in hell outweighs any advantage of believing otherwise", and this proof is nothing less than the use of the evidentialist methodology on the basis of the tripartite factors discussed above.

3. Evidentialism in Practice

To further illustrate the evidentialist method, we shall apply it to prove religious belief. The use of evidentialism for proving the prophethood of a claimant to prophecy requires us to examine the sum of the evidence which is indicative of the veracity of the claimant's claim to prophethood. These can include glad tidings given by prophets in the past concerning him, his sincerity and honesty, his miracles, the conformance or absence of conflict of his teachings with reason and common sense, and the positive impact of his teachings on the reformation of the individual and on the social life of humanity as a whole.

The evaluation of all these indications can lead to certain knowledge about the veracity of a claimant's claim, even though it is possible that each of the indications taken by themselves (without their integration into a whole) do not provide certainty and therefore do not have scientific standing and authority. The evidence of the credibility of the evidentialist method in this example is the following: if someone puts forward a claim to prophethood and performs a miracle (such as opening the Red Sea, like Moses , or curing the blind, as in the case of Jesus the Christ), but fails to fulfill the other requirements or some of them (especially his sincerity and honesty and the absence of conflict of his teachings with reason and common sense), then certainty in his prophethood will not obtain. Without a doubt the two indicators of sincerity and honesty and the absence of conflict of one's teachings with reason and common sense play a central role in proving the prophethood of a claimant to prophecy. No reasonable person will accept the claim to prophethood of a person who is not possessed of a sound moral character or one whose teachings go against the demands of reason, even if such a person were to part the sea or cure the blind. This point speaks to the fact that miracles alone cannot provide sufficient grounds for proving a prophet's prophethood and can only do so when they are integrated with other indicators so that the evidence is evaluated as a whole, i.e. by way of an evidentialist methodology. Therefore, the methodology of those who seek to examine these kinds of evidence in isolation and evaluate each indication to prophethood individually and without taking the other indicators into account (and ultimately determining some to be valid and others to be invalid) is at variance with the evidentialist perspective and is therefore deficient.

By paying due attention to one's own life and the life of others it becomes clear that the methodology known as "evidentialism" is the method used by wise men universally and throughout the whole of history and across all cultures. Ordinary rational people throughout the world attain belief in various propositions through this same method in their private and public lives as well as in their personal beliefs and therefore either act on those beliefs or reject them.

The above presentation of the case for evidentialism as a methodology will have to suffice for our purposes as we do not have the room in this volume to do an exhaustive comparative analysis between the evidentialist approach and other epistemological approaches. This would require a full volume in its own right.

2 The Application of Evidentialism in Proofs of the Imāmate

A sequence of historical evidence indicates that the twelve Imāms of Shī'a Islam, i.e. Alī b. Abī-Tāleb ﷺ and the eleven Imāms from his progeny ﷺ were the rightful successors of the Prophet ﷺ and were vested in the office of the imāmate by way of divine designation. While it is possible that each of these historical indications taken on their own might not provide an unassailable case for such a claim, taken together, they will indeed lead to this conclusion.

There is abundant historical evidence that proves the right of the Shī'a Imāms to the Imāmate. Shī'a scholars have explicated many of these proofs in their various works. The objective of this essay is not to provide a repetitive compilation of this evidence; rather, the aim is to give expression to a specific indication and proof which apparently has hitherto been neglected. The explication of this particular proof can be done either independently or in combination with other proofs. Here we shall proceed with the second option, such that this proof is presented alongside two other scriptural proofs.

17

In this chapter, we will first present two scriptural indicators or proofs in brief, and in Chapter Three, we will provide a detailed demonstration of the historical and rational proof which is the main substance of this essay.

1: Twelve Princes from the Progeny of Ishmael

In the Old Testament of the Bible which is accepted by Jews and Christians alike, after giving glad tidings to Abraham concerning the birth of his second son Isaac, and Abraham's supplications concerning his first-born son Ishmael, God ﷻ addresses Abraham stating:

> (Genesis 17:20 KJV) And as for Ishmael, I have heard thee: Behold, I have blessed him, and will make him fruitful, and will multiply him exceedingly; twelve princes shall he beget, and I will make him a great nation.[9]

In this verse, glad tidings are given of the birth of twelve persons from the progeny of Ishmael who are characterized as being "princes" or "rulers", and are not described as being prophets, as people of knowledge nor people who will be known for their practice of their worship of God ﷻ. Thus, according to the Holy Bible, the defining characteristic of these "princes" and "rulers" is the leadership of the community of those who have attained to faith in God ﷻ, or, in other words, the imāmate. The other attribute of this group as a whole is that they are twelve in number.

Ishmael lived in the land of the Hejāz in the vicinity of the Ka'ba,[10] and a branch of the Arabs arose from his stock. Thus, in order to find these twelve princes, we must look to the Arabs in the Hejāz among the progeny of Ishmael, rather than to the tribes of Israel who were the sons of Isaac and Jacob and who lived in the Levant and Egypt.

2 The Application of Evidentialism in Proofs of the Imāmate

The number twelve which makes its appearance in the Holy Bible is significant; such that the number of persons from the seed of Ishmael who attain to the position of leader or imam must be exactly twelve, no more and no less. It is not logical to suppose that the identity of these twelve persons who are destined to substantiate the realization of this glad tiding is left to the personal tastes and whims of those to whom the Holy Book is addressed, so that each person is free to make up a list of his own liking from the great men of the progeny of Ishmael who have made their appearance throughout the course of history, and for each person to consider their own list to be comprised of those people who are the fulfillment of the prophecy. Rather, it is more fitting that the realization of the number twelve be endowed with a unique attribute which acts to prevent any ambiguity from arising in the message of the Holy Book which could become the basis of deviations of belief, which would in turn engender false instances of supposed fulfillments of the prophecy. At the same time, history does not report any clear example of twelve great leaders (or "princes") among the progeny of Ishmael concerning whom the number twelve has a unique characteristic which separates them from the rest of the field, other than the Imams of the Shī'a, all of whom are great men who were selected from the progeny of Ishmael and whose number is indeed twelve. Additionally, their fulfillment is based on brotherly or filial relationships; and the uninterrupted series that is formed by this special relationship separates them from false contenders for the fulfillment of this prophecy. In other words, these twelve persons must be endowed with a special attribute which separates them from others such that the number twelve becomes manifest in them.

Of course, the name of the immediate sons of Ishmael who are characterized as "princes" appears a few verses down in the Holy Bible;[11] which shows that the Bible has determined the applicability of the twelve princes concerning whom glad tidings have been given in the previous verse. This verse reduces the quantum of possibility of the previous verse's referral to the imāmate of the twelve Imams of the Shīʻa who are from the seed of Ishmael, but it does not eliminate the possibility altogether because it is possible that from the perspective of the Holy Book, the unique instances of the twelve persons from the seed of Ishmael are not those who are named in the second verse. The possibility is therefore left open for other instances to be found in the future to fulfill this prophecy – just as is the case in the Holy Bible with the case of the children of Isaac, where two instances of twelve leaders from the seed of Isaac and in two different times have been specified: firstly, two years after the exodus of the Children of Israel from Egypt into the Sinai desert led by Moses[12]; and secondly, after their arrival in the land of Canaan where they are mentioned in the context of the division of the land.[13] The names specified in each case are at variance with each other, and both groups are described as "leaders". Of course, in the second case, two of the tribes of Israel are excepted because they had already received their share of land, and the Bible specifies the leaders of ten tribes in this case, but then adds the names of these other two, ultimately making the sum add up to twelve.

In any event, by paying due attention to the method of the Bible that specifies the twelve leaders of the tribes of Israel, a strong possibility exists that the fulfillment of the prophecy concerning twelve leaders from the seed of Israel is not limited to that which has already been mentioned in the Holy Book. In the case of the twelve children who are to be the offspring of Ishmael, as with the twelve princes from the progeny of Jacob, the possibility exists for there to be another instance which is not mentioned and that the Bible has only given glad tidings of their birth in some time in the future.

2: Twelve Successors (khalīfa) after the Prophet

The most authoritative scriptural sources[14] from within the Sunni tradition (such as the *Sahīh* of Bokhārī, the *Sahīh* of Muslim, the *Sahīh* of Termedhī,

2 The Application of Evidentialism in Proofs of the Imāmate

the Sonan of Abū-Dāwūd, the *Masnad* of Ahmad b. Hanbal, and the *Masnad* of Tayālasī, and numerous other authoritative scriptural and historical sources from within the Sunni tradition) have related with numerous provenance titles (*asnād*) and by way of many eye witnesses (*sahāba*) that the Prophet ﷺ said:

لايَزَالُ الدِينُ قائماً حتّى تَقُومَ الساعةُ أو يَكُونَ عَلَيكُم اثناعَشَرَ خَليفةً كُلُّهُم مِن قُرَيشٍ.[15]

"This religion will last until the Day of Resurrection, or until such a time that twelve caliphs [other versions have 'Imāms'; the meaning is the same in this context: leader; ruler], all of whom shall be of [the clan of] Quraysh, shall rule over you."

The above hadīth report appears in the *Sahīh* of Muslim (related by Jāber b. Samara). The text varies slightly in each of the reports which appear in the various Sunni hadīth compilations and chronicles of history. However, the meaning is exactly the same, and they all share in common the glad tiding given by the Prophet ﷺ concerning the "twelve successors" that are to follow in his wake. A contemporary researcher has compiled all of the hadīth reports which appear in Sunni sources concerning this prophecy and relates 151 reports gleaned from dozens of Sunnite sources, all of which contain reports of the Prophet ﷺ prophesying the coming of "twelve successors" after him.[16] Similar reports containing the same content are also reported from the Most Noble Prophet ﷺ in various Shī'a scriptural sources.[17]

Considering the superfluity of the authoritative provenance titles (*asnād*) which appear in Sunnite sources, the great scholars of the science of hadīth in the Sunni community have not seen fit to question the authenticity of this report. Rather, some of them have proceeded to explain the report, attempting to determine the identity of the Prophet's ﷺ twelve successors.[18] Much has been written by these scholars concerning this issue, but they have not arrived at a consensus of opinion in this regard. The Sunnite scholars who have attempted to determine the identity of the twelve successors to the Prophet ﷺ which he has prophesied have become daunted and bewildered at the task, and all of the explanations proposed are neither credible nor reliable. Each of these scholars has gathered a list of twelve rulers who have appeared after the passing of the Prophet ﷺ based on their own personal tastes and inclinations, and how each of them has arrived at the number twelve is not based on a unique characteristic which makes the candidates stand out from among the rest of the contenders in the field. A detailed examination and proof of this point would require another book-length essay in and of itself, and falls outside the aim of this book. Shī'a scholarship has produced some valuable research in this area which the interested reader can refer to in order to familiarize his- or herself with Sunnite opinion and their points of weakness.[19] In determining the correct referents of this ḥadīth report, it is necessary to note that just as in the glad tidings given in the Holy Bible, the number twelve is endowed with a particular signification in that the group of persons which is intended by this prophecy is comprised of no more and no less than twelve persons, so that one's search must be focused on a grouping which is comprised of this number and whose members stand out from the rest. Additionally, each of whose individual characteristics as well as the way in which they relate to each other leaves no room for any addition or subtraction from the number twelve.

Given the fact that there are no clear cases in point in the various religio-legal rites (*madhhabs*) within Islam that fit the bill other than that of the Imāmī or Twelver Shī'a rite. Also given that there are no groupings of twelve persons other than the twelve Imams of the Shī'a wherein the number twelve plays a significant role and cannot be added to or subtracted from (without affecting the integrity of the group), it can be concluded that the twelve Imams of the

Shī'a can be a clear fulfillment of the prophecy contained in this hadīth report.

3: Twelve Great Personages in One Uninterrupted Chain

The unprecedented nature of the proof proffered in this essay is grounded in the confidence that is placed in this intellectually and historically supported indicator, which is able to be presented as an independent proof in its own right. However, before we proceed to its demonstration, a preliminary discussion is necessary.

In any given branch of the development and perfection of humanity, great men can be found distributed throughout history among the many nations, races, ethnicities and religions. Great scientists in various scientific fields of endeavor, and great mystics and sages and those whose place is in the peaks of perfection of moral refinement and ethical conduct – the gathering of these is not limited to a specific era or to a special race. While it might be true that some of the attributes of the great personages of history are inherited by their progeny. However, this phenomenon is by no means guaranteed always to occur nor to occur in every instance. Additionally, most of the characteristics of these kinds of people are acquired and are borne out of a personal effort on their part and can therefore not be inherited. It is for this reason that when we refer to history it is plain for all to see that the greatness and genius of great men throughout history in every filed – be it scientific, practical or moral – are generally not transferred to their offspring, and that genius is distributed [more or less evenly] throughout different nations, religions and eras.

Thus it can be said that the possibility of the offspring of a great scientist also becoming a great scientist in his own generation is low, and that the possibility of the great scientist's grandchild becoming another great scientist (in addition to his grandfather and father) is lower still. In any given branch of the sciences, this occurrence might occur, to be sure, but it is a rarity. If we consider the intergenerational chain of scientists of one or two generations and extend this to twelve generations, then we are confronted with a historically extra-ordinary phenomenon that has no precedent whatsoever throughout the length and breadth of history or in any of the branches of the science or the arts and humanities. Imagine twelve physicists like Newton or twelve poets like Hāfez[20] positioned in series in an uninterrupted chain, all of whom have a brotherly or filial relationship with each other. Such a fanciful thought has never had any analogue in the history of humanity's existence.

This preamble having been said, let us now go and scout out the historical record and determine whether or not such an extra-ordinary phenomenon existed with respect to the eleven[21] Imams of the Shī'a. The reason for excepting the twelfth imam from our investigation is that he did not live among the people and lived covertly from the very beginning of his life. Additionally, after attaining to the office of the imāmate during his childhood, his state of occultation began. Therefore, there should not be an expectation that there be copious historical reports at hand concerning his scientific and practical achievements.

In investigating the historical record concerning the Shī'a Imams, it is important to bear the following points in mind, as these points add to the extra-ordinary nature of the unique totality of the Shī'a Imams.

2 The Application of Evidentialism in Proofs of the Imāmate

1. In this investigation of the historical record, we have limited ourselves only to those reports which have been reported by Sunni historians and scholars. We have refrained from reporting what Shī'a historians and scholars have had to say about their own Imams, as one cannot dispel the possibility that might occur in the minds of non-Shī'a researchers that the Shī'a, just like the people of any other sect or religion, might have [unconcious or concious] biases in favor of their leadership which would lead them to exaggerate their excellences and to pass over their faults.

2. The Sunni community does not acknowledge the Imams of the Shī'a to be immaculate (*ma'sūm* = inerrant as well as sinless in Shī'ī belief) or to have an intrinsic connection with the Domain of the Invisible (*ālam-e ghayb*: the metaphysical hypostasis; the underlying substantive domain that is beyond the ken of ordinary human perception), considering them to be normal human beings. If this were not the case, their admissions or disclosures concerning the Imams of the Shī'a would not provide for strong witnesses and warrants for the occurrence of this extra-ordinary phenomenon in human history. In other words, the historians within the Sunni community have no preconceived notions or dogmatic beliefs concerning the Shī'a Imams that would bias their historical reports in favor of these eleven individuals. Rather, their reporting is based on how each of the Imams interacted with the community at large and how their behavior was a manifestation of their character.

3. In the past, and especially during the reigns of the Omayyad and Abbāsid dynasties, the Sunni community's view of the Shī'a was extremely negative, and history has been a sad witness to the countless conflicts between the followers of these two rites throughout the centuries. In such an atmosphere of aggression and enmity (or at a minimum, one of an extreme difference of sectarian opinion), the admissions of Sunnite scholars to the greatness of the Shī'a Imams' learning and to the greatness of their moral character and

standing is telling. It is a shining testimony to the truth that the extent of the greatness of the Shī'a Imams' learning and moral standing was so evident and obvious that it passed the threshold of deniability even to the point where their enemies testified to it. The coincidence of these two conflicting behaviors of the Sunnite scholars, i.e. the scorn and condemnation of the Shī'a on one hand, and the praise and acclamation of their leadership on the other, is an astonishing phenomenon the likes of which are difficult to come by in the annals of history.

4. Not only did the rulers who reigned during the time of the presence of the Shī'a Imams not have a peaceful relationship with them, their relations were difficult at best and would at times break out into open enmity. What bears witness to this, in addition to the tens of authenticated reports of their harassment, imprisonment and exile at the hands of these tyrants, is the martyrdom of the Imams themselves at the hands of the Omayyad and Abbāsid brutes. Therefore, not only was there no quarter provided by the ruling powers that would allow or enable any Shī'a propaganda in promotion of their Imams; rather, there was a concerted and sustained effort on the part of the authorities to slander and defame the character of the Imams and to destroy their reputation. There exist numerous historical accounts of the forging of hadīth reports against the House of the Prophet ﷺ, and of the cursing and imprecation from the pulpits and in the sermons of the Friday communal devotions at the behest and direct orders of the rulers of the day; this was especially the case during the Omayyad period. In such a hostile psychological climate arrayed against the Shī'a Imams, the confession of the majority of the Sunnite scholarly community and on their account of the Sunni community at large to the greatness of the learning of the Imams and to their outstanding moral character and piety is a resounding testimony that speaks volumes for the undeniable greatness of their character.

5. Almost all of the scholars from the Sunni community have lauded the greatness of the Shī'a Imams' learning, moral character and piety. In the view of the scholars from the Sunni community, the Shī'a Imams excelled in the two spheres of thought and action, and again in the view of Sunni scholarship, their actions had reached the peak of perfection both with respect to their piety and their devotional duties toward God, as well as with respect to their duties towards their fellow man. Thus, as admitted by the Sunni community, the Shī'a Imams had reached the peaks of perfection in every human dimension. This point adds to the exceptional position of the Shī'a Imams in human history because normally genius strikes in one dimension of human aptitude, whereas if eleven people in one uninterrupted chain generation after generation are at the peak of perfection in their respective generations in both the greatness of their learning and their practice, and that this is admitted to by their enemies, this is something that is a completely unprecedented phenomenon of history, and is a resounding testimony to the truth that this phenomenon is not the result of normally-occurring natural causes, and must be something that is inspired by Heaven.

Taking the above-mentioned points into account elevates the claim to rightfulness of the twelve Shī'a Imams on the basis of this factor. That said, we shall now proceed to the examination of the views of Sunni scholarship concerning the Shī'a Imams.

The entirety of the Sunni community, and especially their scholarly class, have a great liking for the first three Imams and have praised them profusely. In addition to the greatness of the outstanding character of these three Imams, the reason for this love and admiration goes back to hadīth reports which reporters from within the Sunni community have related from the Prophet of God concerning the excellences of these three Imams. But it seems that other than one hadīth report where the Prophet refers to the fourth Imam as Lord of the Devotees[22] (*seyyed ol-ābedīn*) and a hadīth report where the Prophet ﷺ gives glad tidings to some people concerning their meeting with the fifth Imam, Imam Muhammad al-Bāqer[23], as well as a hadīth report concerning the virtues of making pilgrimage to the shrine of the eighth Imam, Imam Reḍā[24], no other hadīth reports have been transmitted from the Prophet ﷺ about the Imams. Thus, the source of the love and admiration of the scholars of the Sunni community for the first three Imams goes back [at least in part] to hadīth reports related from the Prophet ﷺ of God ﷻ concerning the excellences of these three Imams and the facts concerning the way they lived their lives, and the love and admiration of the Sunni community concerning the rest of the Imams have to do solely with the facts of their lives and how they lived.

Some scholars of the Sunni community have stipulated the greatness of the Members of this House and to their extraordinary uniqueness.

Ahmad b. Abdollāh 'Ajlī (d. 261 AH[25]), one of the earliest biographers, states: "Ja'far b. Muhammad b. Ali b. Hosayn b. Ali b. Abī Tāleb are five imams who have excellences and virtues with which no one else has been endowed."[26] {Edited to this point}

The great scholar and man of letters Allama Hosayn b. Muhammad ar-Rāqeb al-Isfahānī (d. 502 AH) states: "There does not exist on earth five noble people in an uninterrupted generational series concerning whom hadīth reports have been related, other than Ja'far b. Muhammad b. Ali b. Hosayn b. Ali b. Abī Tāleb, may God ﷻ grant all of them His Heaven."[27]

Shamsoddīn Dhahabī (d. 747 AH), one of the greatest historians, prosopographers (*dāneshmandān-e elm-e rejāl*) and biographers of Sunni scholarship confesses in one of his works (after refuting the Shī'a belief in the immaculacy of their Imāms) that while it is true that we do not consider them to be sinless and inerrant, but we certainly admit to their greatness and lofty

2 The Application of Evidentialism in Proofs of the Imāmate

stature. He goes on to say, "Our master (*mowlā*) Alī b. Abī-Ṭāleb ﷺ is one of the Rightly Guided (*rāshedūn*) Caliphs concerning whom the Prophet ﷺ testified that he would attain to Heaven. We People of the Sunna (*ahl as-sunnaʿ*) love him very much, but we do not claim that he is immaculate (*maʿsūm*), nor do we consider Abū-Bakr to be immaculate. Alī b. Abī-Ṭāleb's ﷺ two sons, al-Hasan ﷺ and al-Hosayn ﷺ are the grandsons of the Prophet ﷺ who are the "princes of the youth of paradise".[28] If these two had attained to the office of the caliphate, they would have been worthy of that office.[29] Then comes [Imam] Zeyn ol-Ābedīn ﷺ, who has a high standing and is among the select within the world of scholarship. He [too] was worthy of the office of the leadership of the community. Within the community of believers there were others like him. There are some who own to more fatwas[30] and hadīth reports than him. Similarly, his son, Abū-Jaʿfar [Muhammad] al-Bāqer ﷺ [the fifth Imam], was a great man, was a leader (*imām*), and a *faqīh* (doctor of jurisprudence, Islamic theology and theosophy). He too was worthy of the caliphate [i.e. leadership of the community] and had copious knowledge and learning. And his son, [the sixth Imam] Jaʿfar as-Sādeq ﷺ, who was endowed with a high [spiritual] station and was a leader [of the people]. He too was worthy of the caliphate and was more worthy of this office than al-Mansūr (Dawānaqī), the caliph of his era. Similarly, his son [the seventh Imam] Mūsā al-Kāzem, who was endowed with a high [spiritual] station and had copious knowledge and learning. He too was more worthy of the caliphate than Hārūn or-Rashīd. There were others who were like him in nobility and virtue. Then his son [the eighth Imam] Ali b. Mūsā ar-Reḍā ﷺ, who was endowed with a high [spiritual] station and had copious knowledge and learning; he was a gifted orator and was a powerful speaker with a great power to influence the souls and spirits of others. [The Caliph] Ma'mūn made him his heir apparent on account of the greatness of his august character. He died in the year 203 AH. His son Muhammad Jawād ﷺ was also one of the great men of his nation, although he did not reach the heights of his father in knowledge of the religious sciences. Similarly, his son al-Hādī

, who was a great and pious man, and his son Hasan al-Askarī ﷺ was likewise [such a man]; may God ﷻ have mercy on all their souls."³¹

In these concise words, Dhahabī admits to the lofty station of the eleventh Imam in terms of his learning and piety, and states concerning most of them that they were worthy of the office of leadership (*khilāfa*) of the entire community and to the succession of the Prophet ﷺ in their own eras. This admission of the great scholar could indeed be an unintended confession to the effect that the twelve Imams of the Shī'a are indeed what was intended by the Prophet ﷺ as reported in the authoritative hadīth of "the Twelve Caliphs (*khilāfa*)".

The renowned Shāfi'ī Mo'tazelī scholar Eben Abī'l-Hadīd (d. 656 AH) states in his great commentary on the *Nahj ol-Balāgha*: "Where can one find anyone – either from within or from without [the tribe of] Quraysh – the likes of the sons of Abū-Tāleb? Ten people like unto each other. Each one a scholar, an ascetic, pious, brave, gracious, pure and refined. Some of whom attained to the office of the leadership of the community, and others to the heir apparancy. An [uninterrupted] chain from father to son ten generations long, which consists of Hasan ﷺ the son of Ali, the son of Muhammad, the son of Ali, the son of Mūsā, the son of Ja'far, the son of Muhammad, the son of Ali, the son of Hosayn, the son of Ali ﷺ, and nowhere has such virtue been gathered in a single family anywhere, be they Arab or non-Arab."³²

Shaykh Abdollāh b. Muhammad b. 'Āmer Shabrāwī ash-Shāfe'ī (d. 1172 AH), a professor at the al-Azhar university [in Cairo] says: "The titles of Imām Muhammad al-Hojja' ﷺ [the twelfth Imām] consist of al-Mahdī, al-Qāem, al-Montazer, al-Khalaf as-Sāleh, and Sāheb oz-Zamān, the most well-known of which is al-Mahdī ﷺ. For this reason, the Shī'a consider him to be the fulfillment of a *sahīh* (sound, authoritative) hadīth which states that he [the Mahdī ﷺ, i.e. the Guided One] will appear at the end of time, and that he is in [= was last seen entering] a cold-cellar in Sāmarrā, and had entered into it, and the Shīʿa have written books about this issue; but this is incorrect, and the Mahdī concerning whom we have sahīh hadīth reports and who will make his appearance at the end of time is someone other than he [whom the Shīʿa believe to be the one], irrespective of the fact that his [the person the Shīʿa believe to be the Mahdī ﷺ] lineage is the most noble and munificent [of lineages], but like everyone else, he was born and grew up and is not one whose life is [extra-ordinarily] long. The light of this Hāshemite House[33] and the purified prophetic lineage and the company of Ālids[34] has become universal, and they are twelve Imams whose virtues excel [all (?) others], whose attributes are luminous, whose souls are noble, and whose lineage is Muhammadan and munificent, and they consist of the following: Ali b. Abu Talib, Hasan b. Ali, Husain b. Ali, Ali b. Husain, Muhammad b. Ali, Ja'far b. Muhammad, Musa b. Ja'far, Ali b. Musa, Muhammad b. Ali, Ali b. Muhammad, Hasan b. Ali, and Muhammad b. Hasan, may God ﷻ be please with all of them."[35]

Shaykh Muhammad Abū-Zahra (d. 1394 AH), also a professor at the al-Azhar university and one of the greatest and most prolific scholars of the Islamic sciences of his era, says: "[Imam] Jaʿfar as-Sādeq , is an Imam and son of an Imam, and this chain [of successive Imams] continues back through their fathers to Alī b. Abī-Tāleb ... a noble and munificent House. We do not claim that knowledge is inheritable, but we do say that lineage and breeding are not without their effects. [Imam Jaʿfar as-Sādeq ﷺ was] a man who grew up in a house of wisdom (ʿilm; knowledge, science) who inherited knowledge from one great [man, who in turn inherited it] from another great [man of knowledge and wisdom]. He has a passion for it and is [naturally or innately] oriented to it [literally, "turns toward it"]. If he found the environment to be conducive and had the opportunity for the acquisition of knowledge and there were no hindrances to impede his acquisition of knowledge, in such a case, [his quest for] knowledge will bear fruit."[36]

Shaykh Muhammad Kheḍr Hosayn, another professor at the al-Azhar university says: "[Imam] Muhammad al-Bāqer ﷺ is the fifth Imam of the twelve Imams in whom the Shī'a believe, which is why they are called "Twelvers". These Imams ﷺ consist of the following: Ali b. Abu Talib, Hasan b. Ali, Husain b. Ali, Ali b. Husain, Muhammad b. Ali, Ja'far b. Muhammad, Musa b. Ja'far, Ali b. Musa, Muhammad b. Ali, Ali b. Muhammad, Hasan b. Ali, and Muhammad b. Hasan. The last person is considered by the Shī'a to be the awaited Mahdī... The Sunni position concerning these twelve Imams is that [all] attained to the [lofty] station of knowledge and piety."[37]

Shaykh ol-Islam Muhammad Abo'l-Hādī b. Hasan as-Sayyādī ar-Refā'ī (d. 1327 AH) states: "Muslims the world over know that the chiefs of the *owlīā* (those who have spiritual proximity to God ﷻ) and the chosen leaders after Alī b. Abī-Tāleb ﷺ are of his lineage and are his pure progeny. An uninterrupted chain from one generation to the next up to the present time, and they are without any doubt the chiefs of the *owlīā* (those who have spiritual proximity to God ﷻ) and the chiefs of the *owlīā* of the *owlīā*. They are the leaders who lead the saints (*owlīā*) toward the Divine Presence, and they are free of any and all impurity and defect. Who [else can one find] among the first generation of *owlīā* after the class of the Companions of the Prophet ﷺ [who have a spiritual caliber] like unto [that of] al-Hasan ﷺ [the second Imam] and al-Hosayn ﷺ [the third Imam] and al-Bāqer ﷺ [the fifth Imam], and al-Kāzem ﷺ [the seventh Imam], and as-Sādeq ﷺ [the sixth Imam], and at-Taqī al-Jawād ﷺ [the ninth Imam], and an-Naqī ﷺ [the tenth Imam], and al-Askarī ﷺ [the eleventh Imam]?"[38]

The literary corpus of the Sunnites from the past up to the present is full of praise and profuse acclaim for the Imams of the Shī'a. The compilation of these instances would necessitate the production of a multi-volume work.[39]

2 The Application of Evidentialism in Proofs of the Imāmate

Now while it is true that the scholars of the Sunni community as a whole have praised the Imams after Imam Hosayn profusely, their acquaintance with them is not uniform; and this heterogeny has to do with the variations in the social and political conditions at the time of each of these Imams. We will thus provide a short report of the conditions that obtained from the time of the fourth Imam onward, so that the reasons for the variations in recognition and acclamation of Sunnite scholarship is clarified.

After the martyrdom of Imam Hosayn and the uprisings of the Penitent movement (*tawwābūn*) and of Mokhtār ath-Thaqafī (both of which were aftershocks of that terrible event [of Ashura]), the Omayyads realized that violent repression of the Shī'a Imams entailed costly consequences for their regime. Thus they changed their policy and were less severe in their dealings with Imam Zeynol-Abedīn. Additionally, the fact that Medina (where the Imam lived) was a long distance from Damascus (the capital of the Omayyads) provided some leeway for the limited non-political activities of the Imam in Medina.

In those days and for years afterwards, Medina was the spiritual and cultural capital of the world of Islam, and the greatest scholars of the Islamic sciences were domiciled there. The slight latitude that had opened up for Imam Sajjād[40] (as) gave his eminence the opportunity to proceed, to the extent possible, to the guidance of the people. It is possible to get a glimpse of the years that this great man expended carrying out this effort by reading what has been written about him by the greatest of the *tābe'īn*[41] and scholars of that era. These reports inform us of the deep impact that the Imam had on the great men of that era such as Zohrī, Mālek b. Anas, Yahyā b. Sa'īd, Abū Hāzem, Zeyd b. Aslam, and others.

The opportunity that had opened up in the time of Imam Zeyn ol-Abedīn ﷺ continued and greatly expanded during the time of Imam Bāqer ﷺ. The dynastic change from the Omayyads to the Abbāsids which occurred at the time of Imam Bāqer ﷺ and the events surrounding the clash of these two dynasties who were vying for power meant that the rulers whose reigns were contemporaneous with the imamates of Imam Bāqer ﷺ and Imam Sādeq ﷺ necessarily had to neglect their monitoring and control of the activities of these two Imams as the coming to power of the Abbāsids and their consolidation of their powerbase took up all of their energies. Thus Imam Bāqer ﷺ and even more so, Imam Sādeq ﷺ were able to make the most of the opportunity that presented itself, and did so by maximizing their efforts in propagating the authentic religious teachings of Islam and by educating and cultivating a new class of Muslims in accordance with those teachings. The exceptional circumstance, i.e. the relative let-up of the systematic repression of the Imams of the House of the Prophet ﷺ, gave rise to the renown of the two Imams throughout all the dominions of Islam for their knowledge and their piety, the first of whom became known as Bāqer ol-Olūm (the Splitter of [the kernel of] Knowledge), and the second of whom came to be known as as-Sādeq (the Truthful One, or the one who always speaks the truth). This in turn gave rise to a wave of migration from the corners of the realms of Islam by those seeking knowledge of the Islamic sciences to Medina so that they could study Islam at the feet of these two Imams – all of which will be explored when we turn to the reports of the Sunni scholars concerning these two Imams.

After completely vanquishing the last traces of the Omayyads and completing the consolidation of their own rule, the Abbāsid rulers became aware of the unique position which the Imams of the Shī'a enjoyed among the Muslim populace, and the danger which this posed to them. Consequently, they changed their way of dealing with them. A clear example of this change of policy was the harsh way in which they dealt with the seventh Imam, Imam Mūsā al-Kāzem ﷺ, which included his forced change of domicile from Medina to Baghdad (which was the new capital of the Abbāsids), and the long periods of imprisonment which the Imam had to endure in the dungeons of the Abbāsids.

After the martyrdom of Imam Mūsā al-Kāzem ﷺ, and the death of Hārūn, the Abbāsid caliph, his wily successor inaugurated a new method for limiting and controlling the influence of the Imam. He invited the eighth Imam, Imam Alī ar-Reḍā ﷺ to his capital and tried to weaken the Imam's appeal to the people by posing him as a contender and challenger to the throne of rulership. But the superb character of Imam Reḍā ﷺ and the prudent precautionary measures he took foiled Ma'mūn's plot, and once more, the Imam of the Shī'a was able to avail himself of the opportunity which this new condition provided to propagate the authentic teachings of Islam, and in so doing, enamored the hearts of the people to himself and made a name for himself outside of his immediate circle of partisans.

Having experimented and experienced various other methods of dealing with the leaders of the Shī'a, the Abbāsid regime gradually returned back to the tried and tested method of harsh suppression. Thus, they transferred the Imams from Medina to the capital where they kept them under house arrest and under the strictest possible control, and ultimately, resorted to their physical elimination in their youth in order to eliminate the danger that their existence posed to the caliphal regime. A consequence of this policy was the premature martyrdom of Imam al-Jawād at-Taqī ﷺ, the ninth Imam, at the age of 25 at the hands of the forces of the caliph al-Mo'tasem, and the martyrdom of Imam al-Hādī ﷺ, the tenth Imam, at the age of 41, and the martyrdom of Imam Hasan al-Askarī ﷺ, the eleventh Imam, at the age of 28. These three Imams had the shortest lifespans among all of the Imams of the Shī'a, and during these short lifespans the caliphs did not let up on any of their repressive measures, severely restricting the people's access to their Imams by keeping them under house arrest and forcing them into exile to a garrison town (*askarīya*)[42] 100 km or so north of Baghdad where they were kept in isolation. All these measures were taken in the service of their policy of preventing the luminous personalities of the Imams from seeing the light of day among the Muslim populace over whom they forced their tyrannical reign.

Unfortunately, this method of brute force was successful, and because of the short lifespans of these three Imams and the policy of keeping them in strict isolation, the Muslim masses were not able to become as familiar with their august personalities and benefit from their knowledge as they had benefitted from their fathers and forefathers before them. Thus, one should not expect the historical reports which have reached us from the Sunni scholars who were contemporaneous with these last three Imams to be as numerous as the reports about the Imams who preceded them.

3 The Evidence

Let us now proceed to an examination of what some of the great Sunni scholars have said concerning the twelve Imams, as well as what some non-Muslim notables have had to say about them, starting with the first Imam, Imam Alī b. Abī-Tāleb ﷺ.

1. Imam Ali b. Abī-Tāleb

Hundreds of hadīth reports from the Prophet ﷺ have been related in the Sunni sources concerning the various virtues of Imam Ali ﷺ. A group of Shi'a scholars has worked on compiling these reports and has produced voluminous books on the subject, some of which were already referred to. The copious volume of these reports and the authority and reliability of them taken in their totality is known to every Muslim, be he Sunni or Shi'a, both groups of whom are united in their evaluation of the greatness of his character on the basis of these reports.

We will not be reviewing these reports in their entirety (as this is beyond the scope of this essay); rather, what we will be presenting is a small but representative sample of what the great scholars and notable men of the Sunni community have had to say concerning Imam Ali ﷺ, as well as a sampling of the opinion of non-Muslims, all of which will cover the period from the era of the Associates of the Prophet ﷺ up to the present day.

Sunni scholarship considers Imam Ali ؑ to be the last of the "Rightly-Guided" Caliphs.[43] In Sunni opinion, the Rightly-Guided caliphs were the best of people after the Prophet ﷺ, in the order of Abu Bakr, and then Omar, after which there is a difference of opinion between them concerning the question as to whether Othmān is preeminent to Ali ؑ or vice versa, or whether they both occupy the same spiritual rank. Most of them have opted for the first position.[44] Hasan al-Basrī (d. 110 AH), a scholar from the *tābe'īn* generation,[45] chose the second option (i.e. the preeminence of Imam Ali ؑ).[46] Thus, in the opinion of most of the scholars from the Sunni community, Imam Ali ؑ is the third or fourth most prominent personality within the world of Islam after the Prophet ﷺ himself. We hasten to add that notwithstanding this position, the majority of the Mo'tazelite Sunnis[47] were of the opinion that Imam Ali ؑ was preeminent over the other three caliphs and is the first most prominent personality within the world of Islam after the Prophet ﷺ; examples of those who held this position include al-Eskāfī al-Mo'tazelī (d. 240 AH), Abol-Hasan ar-Rammānī (d. 384 AH), and Eben Abi'l-Hadīd ash-Shāfe'ī (d. 656 AH).[48] This opinion was also shared by the Abāsid caliph al-Ma'mūn.[49] Eben Abi'l-Hadīd writes:

[Imam] Ali was more deserving of the office of the succession [to the Prophet ﷺ] (*khelāfat*), but [this was] not on account of a specific [divine] investiture to succession (*an-nass*) on the part of God ﷻ or His Prophet ﷺ; rather, [this was] on account of his preeminence over others. He was the greatest person after the Prophet ﷺ of God ﷻ, and was more deserving of the caliphate than any other Muslim, but he forewent his right as an expedient measure in order that the cause (*amr*) of Islam would not suffer damage [as a result of a civil war which would undoubtedly have ensued had he insisted on his right], and in order thereby to ensure that the truth [i.e.

3 The Evidence

the teachings of Islam] be dispersed [unmolested by a civil war]; and this is because the Arabs were envious of him and held rancor and resentment in their hearts toward him.[50]

Sunni and non-Muslim scholars have written numerous books on the character and virtues of Imam Ali ﷺ.[51]

A sampling of what the greatest personalities of the Islamic world and of the Sunni community have had to say about Imam Ali follows:

1. One day, Abū Bakr (d. 13 AH), the first caliph, pointing to Ali b. Abī-Tāleb ﷺ said, "Anyone who would be edified to look at the greatest of men, and to the closest of men [to the Prophet ﷺ], and to the most preeminent and the greatest of men should look to this here [person] who just entered."[52]

2. Omar b. al-Khattāb (d. 23 AH), the second caliph, consulted Imam Ali ﷺ concerning the issue of plentitude, and Imam Ali ﷺ would guide him as to how best to deal with this issue. Imam Ali ﷺ would also correct Omar's juridical errors on numerous occasions (all of which have been duly recorded in the annals of the history of those early days). This guidance of Imam Ali's ﷺ prompted Omar to make the following remark concerning his counsellor:
   2.1. "If it were not for Ali ﷺ, Omar would have perished."[53]
   2.2. "The most learned and knowledgeable among us in judgment and in the recitation [i.e. in the correct reading] of the Quran is Ali b. Abī-Tāleb ﷺ."[54]
   2.3. "Ali ﷺ is the most learned [among us] in juridical matters ('alā aqdānā)."[55]
   2.4. "I seek refuge in God ﷻ from all problems in which [recourse to] Abol-Hasan [Ali b. Abī-Tāleb ﷺ] is not available."[56]

39

2.5. "I seek refuge in God ﷻ from living among a people among whom you, O Abol-Hasan [Alī b. Abī-Tāleb ؑ], are not present."⁵⁷

3. Abdollāh b. Mas'ūd (d. 32 AH), who was a great Associate of the Prophet ﷺ and a scholar and exegete of the Quran has stated:
   3.1. "The most informed person in Medina concerning the laws of the Quran and its [proper] reading [literally, 'recitation'] is Alī b. Abī-Tāleb ؑ."⁵⁸
   3.2. The Noble Quran was revealed, (literally, 'descended': *onzila*) in seven modes (*ahrāf*, sing. *harf*). Each mode has an inner and outer aspect, and the inner and outer aspect [of each mode] is with Alī b. Abī-Tāleb ؑ."⁵⁹

4. 'Amr b. Ās (d. 43 AH), the wily vizier of Mo'āwiya, and a die-hard enemy of Imam Ali ؑ states: "None of the Associates (*sahāba*) of the Prophet ﷺ has the virtues of Alī b. Abī-Tāleb ؑ."⁶⁰

5. Sa'd b. Abī-Waqqās (d. 55 AH), an Associate of the Prophet ﷺ and the commander of the Muslim army in its war against the Persians, and one of the members of the Council of Six appointed by Omar to determine his successor, states: "Omar did not appoint anyone to the Council [of Six] without his being worthy of the caliphate. None of us six had a right to the caliphate over the other [five], other than by way of his being selected by the others, whereas Ali ؑ had what [qualifications and virtues which] we had, but we did not have what he had. If Talha and Zobayr remained in their homes [and had not risen up in rebellion against Ali ؑ], it would have been better for them, and may God ﷻ have mercy on the soul of the Mother of the Faithful [*omm ol-mo'menīn*, reference to Āesha, who lead Talha and Zobayr in the first internecine battle of the nascent Muslim community against its leader, Imam Ali ؑ]."⁶¹

6. There are many reports from Āesha (d. 58 AH), one of the wives of the Prophet ﷺ, concerning the greatness of the character of Imam Ali ؏, including:
   6.1. Ali ؏ was the most learned person with respect to the *sunna* (the way of the Most Noble Prophet ﷺ as exemplary model and paradigmatic example) of the Prophet ﷺ."[62]
   6.2. Ali ؏ was the best person, and no one doubts him [i.e. his righteousness] other than an unbeliever (*kāfir*)."[63]
7. Mo'āwiya (d. 70 AH), the first Omayyad caliph had admitted to the excellences of Imam Ali ؏ on numerous occasions even though he went to war against the Imam of the community and was a bitter enemy of his.
   7.1. An example of this praise occurred when he was given news of the Imam's ؏ martyrdom, where he is reported to have said: "Understanding [of the Islamic sciences] (*fiqh*) and knowledge [of the teachings of Islam] (*'ilm*) were lost with the loss of Ali ؏."[64]
   7.2. He is also reported to have said: "May God ﷻ have mercy on Abol-Hasan's [Imam Ali's ؏] soul. He overtook all who went before him [in the excellences of his virtues] and dashed the hopes of all who will follow him, of ever being able to overtake him… Never! Never!! Women are barren in [their inability to] give birth to the like of Ali ؏!"[65]
   7.3. Abdollāh b. Abī-Mihjan ath-Thaqafi came to Mo'āwiya from Imam Ali's ؏ presence and said, "O Commander of the Faithful! I have come from the presence of the son of Abū-Tāleb ؏, who is a dimwitted browbeaten miser!" Mo'āwiya responded, "Do you understand what you are saying?? That you call Ali ؏ a dimwit, I swear [upon my oath] to God ﷻ! If the eloquent speech (literally, 'tongues') of all of the people were to be gathered and to become one voice, [the power of eloquence of] Ali's ؏ oratory will suffice

to match it. Concerning that which you say about him, namely, that he is timid; may your mother sit in mourning at your death!! Have you ever seen anyone go to battle against him and live [to tell the tale]? And concerning that which you say about him, namely, that he is timid; I swear [upon my oath] to God 🕮! If he had two houses, one made of gold and the other of straw, he would give up the gold one before the straw one." The Thaqafite then said, "So why are you at war with him?" Mo'āwiya responded, "Because of [the alleged vengeance for] the blood of Othmān and for this ring [of the caliphate] which endows its bearer with fortune and enables him to see to the needs of his kinfolk and to accumulate wealth for them." The Thaqafite man laughed at Mo'āwiya's speech and went on to join the forces of Imam Ali 🕮 (against Mo'āwiya).

8. Omm Salama (d. 62 AH), one of the wives of the Prophet 🕮, has stated: "Ali was always on the side of *al-haqq* (that which is right; the truth; and that which has ultimate reality; one of the Names and Attributes of God 🕮). Anyone who follows him has followed *al-haqq*, and anyone who abandons him abandons *al-haqq*. This is a pledge from days of old (literally, days before this)."⁶⁶

9. Abdollāh b. Abbās (d. 68 AH), the Prophet's 🕮 cousin, Associate and Quranic exegete, who is known as 'the Scholar of the Community of the Faithful', was a companion, devotee and student of Imam Ali's 🕮. There are many reports of him praising and eulogizing Imam Ali 🕮, such as:

   9.1. "Women are barren in [their inability to] give birth to the like of Ali 🕮! I swear [upon my oath] to God 🕮! I have not seen or heard of a leader such as him."⁶⁷

   9.2. "There are eighteen virtues of Alī b. Abī-Tāleb 🕮 each one of which alone would guarantee him felicity in the hereafter."⁶⁸

9.3. "Alī b. Abī-Tāleb ﷺ has thirteen virtues none of which can be claimed by anyone else in the community of faith."⁶⁹

9.4. "Alī b. Abī-Tāleb ﷺ exceeded others [in excellence] in many affairs which, if one of these was to be divided among all [of God ﷻ] creatures, they would be enveloped in righteousness.⁷⁰

9.5. "The phrase "those who have attained to faith and do good works" does not appear anywhere in the Quran save that it refers to those to whom Alī b. Abī-Tāleb ﷺ is their statesman and leader; neither is there an Associate of the Prophet ﷺ whose mention is made in the Quran only by way of reprimand or reproach by God ﷻ, except Alī b. Abī-Tāleb ﷺ who is only mentioned [in the Quran] by way of praise."⁷¹

9.6. "I swear [upon my oath] to God ﷻ! Nine-tenths of knowledge has been given to Alī b. Abī-Tāleb ﷺ, and I swear [upon my oath] to God ﷻ! He is a partner with the rest of you in the remaining tenth!"⁷²

9.7. Eben Abbās was asked what kind of a man Alī b. Abī-Tāleb ﷺ was. He said, "He was filled with wisdom, knowledge, warrior-nature and courage. He was close to the Prophet ﷺ and believed he would attain to anything he set his mind to; so he attained to everything which he reached for."⁷³

9.8. Eben Abbās was asked how his knowledge measured up against his cousin Alī b. Abī-Tāleb ﷺ. He said, "Like a drop of rain compared to a vast ocean."⁷⁴

9.9. Mo'āwiya asked Eben Abbās, "What is your opinion of Alī b. Abī-Tāleb ﷺ?" Eben Abbās replied, "May God ﷻ have mercy of Abol-Hasan's [Imam Ali's ﷺ] soul. I swear [upon my oath] to God ﷻ! He was the standard of [true] guidance, the cavern of God-wariness and piety (*taqwā*), the locus of acumen, a mountain of splendor, the [guiding] light of those who course through the dark of night, the one who beckons to the greatest objective, the one who knows the [mysteries of the sacred] Primordial Books (*as-sohof al-ūlā*), the upholder of the true meaning of scripture (*ta'wīl*) and of the remembrance and invocation of God ﷻ (*dhikr*), the one who is Proximate to the Ground of Guidance, the expeller of injustice and iniquity, the one who turns [those who will be guided by him] away from paths of destruction, and the best of those who have attained to faith and are endowed with God-wariness and piety (*taqwā*), the Lord of those who don the garb [of pilgrimage], and the most virtuous of those who perform the Major Pilgrimage (*hajj*), the most munificent of those who establish justice; the most eloquent of those who have [ever] dwelled on Earth, other than the [great] prophets and the Chosen Prophet (*al-mostafā*, the chosen, a title of the Most Noble Prophet ﷺ). He is the Lord of the two *qiblas* (directions of prayer, i.e. as the first male adopter of Islam after the Prophet ﷺ, he prayed in the direction of al-Qods before a revelation changed its direction to the Ka'ba). Is there any among those who testify to the unicity of God ﷻ who is better than he, whereas he was the husband of the best of the ladies [of paradise], and the father of the two grandsons of the Prophet ﷺ? My eyes have not set upon the like of him, nor will they ever do so until the Day of the Resurrection. May God ﷻ curse and the curse of [all] His bondsmen be upon any who curse him until the Resurrection."[75]

10. Abdollāh b. Omar (d. 73 AH), the son of the second caliph and an honorable dignitary among the Sunni community, has said:

10.1. "Alī b. Abī-Tāleb ؑ is the most knowledgeable person with respect to that which was revealed to the Prophet ﷺ."[76]

10.2. Abū Hārūn al-'Abdī reports: "I was seated beside Abdollāh b. Omar when Nafi' b. Azraq[77] entered and said, 'I swear [upon my oath] to God ﷻ, I have enmity toward Ali ؑ in my heart.' Abdollāh b. Omar said, 'May God ﷻ hate you! You have enmity toward a man whose excellence of virtue in a single matter is better than the whole world and all that is in it."⁷⁸

11. Jāber b. Abdollāh al-Ansārī (d. 78 AH), the great Associate of the Prophet ﷺ and a devotee of Imam Ali ؑ and of the People of his House states:
    11.1. "Ali ؑ is the best of men in the righteousness of whose cause none but a hypocrite will harbor any doubt."⁷⁹
    11.2. When he was asked his opinion of Imam Ali ؑ, he responded: "He is the best of men. None but an unbeliever will harbor rancor in his heart toward him."⁸⁰

12. Sa'īd b. Mosayyeb (d. 94 AH), the great Medinan scholar of the *tābe'ūn* generation states: "After the Prophet, there was no one more learned than Ali b. Abī-Tāleb ؑ."⁸¹

13. Sha'bī (d. 103 AH), another scholar of the *tābe'ūn* generation states:
    13.1. "Abū Bakr composed poetry, as did Omar; but Ali b. Abī-Tāleb ؑ was better than both of them as a poet."⁸²
    13.2. Concerning Imam Ali ؑ he says, "He was the most generous person. He had a disposition which was pleasing to God ﷻ and which was munificence and generosity."⁸³

14. Mojāhed b. Jabr (d. 104 AH), another great scholar of the *tābe'ūn* generation and a student of Eben Abbās, states: "Ali b. Abī-Tāleb ؑ has seven virtues which none of the Associates of the Prophet ﷺ had; but each and every virtue that the Prophet's ﷺ Associates had, Ali ؑ also had."⁸⁴

15. Hasan al-Basrī (d. 110 AH), the great scholar of the tābeūn generation, was asked his opinion about Imam Ali ؑ. In reply he said,

15.1. "What can I say about him! He exceeded [all the other Associates of the Prophet ﷺ] in the excellence of his virtues, in his knowledge, wisdom, in his understanding of the Quranic sciences (*fiqh*), meditation, his spiritual proximity to the Prophet ﷺ, [as a warrior] in battle and in afflicting [damage to the enemy], his asceticism, his judgeship, and in his kinship with the Prophet ﷺ. Ali ؑ was in a lofty station. May God ﷻ have mercy on his soul and bestow blessings unto him."[85]

15.2. In another report, he is related to have responded to this same question as follows: "I swear [upon my oath] to God ﷻ! Ali b. Abi-Taleb ؑ was an arrow from God ﷻ quiver which was aimed at His enemies and which hit the bullseye. Ali ؑ was a divine among this community of faith, and excelled among the people of this community in his [spiritual] proximity to the Prophet ﷺ. He was not indifferent toward God ﷻ commands, nor was he culpable [in any way] in His religion, nor did he rob Him of His rights. *Ayāt* were revealed about him in the Quran which honored him, and he attained to his peaceful Heaven on their account."[86]

16. 'Atā b. Aslam (d. 114 AH), the great theologian and jurisdoctor of the *tābe'ūn* generation, was asked whether he knew of anyone more knowledgeable [in the teachings of Islam] than Ali b. Abī-Tāleb ؑ. He said, "I swear [upon my oath] to God ﷻ, I do not!"[87]

17. Khalīl b. Ahmad (d. 170 AH), the great litterateur and founder of the science of prosody, describes Imam Ali ؑ in the following terms: "Everyone's dependence on him [i.e. on his knowledge], and his independence from everyone is proof of his being everyone's leader (*imām*)."[88]

18. Imam Shāfe'ī (d. 204 AH), the eponymous founder of the Shāfe'ī religio-legal rite (*madhhab*), always considered himself a devotee and follower of the *ahl al-bayt*, of the People of the House of the Prophet. Some people talked behind his back on this account, and he responded to them as follows: "He told me, 'Have you then become a Rafiḍite?'[89] I said, 'Be quiet! Rejection (*ar-rafaḍ*) is not my religion, nor is it my belief; nonetheless, without a doubt, I will defend the best *imām* (leader) and guide [of my religion]. If the love of the *walī* (friend; he who has spiritual proximity to God) of God is rejectionism, then I am the most rejectionist of His bondsmen."[90]

19. Muhammad b. Wāqedī (d. 207 AH), one of the earliest historians of Islam and author of the famous work al-Maghāzī, writes, "Ali was the miracle of the Prophet, like Moses' staff and the bringing to life of the dead of Jesus the son of Mary."[91]

20. Ahmad b. Hanbal (d. 241 AH), the eponymous founder of the Hanbalī religio-legal rite (*madhhab*) writes concerning Imam Ali as follows: "The virtues which have been reported concerning Ali b. Abī-Ṭāleb are unmatched by any of the Associates of the Prophet of God. Ali b. Abī-Ṭāleb was always with al-haqq (that which is right; the truth; and that which has ultimate reality; one of the Names and Attributes of God), and *al-haqq* was with him (i.e. he was ever in the right), wherever he was."[92]

20.1. Abdollāh, Ahmad b. Hanbal's son, says, "I was seated by my father's side when a group from Karkh came over and talked at length about the reigns (caliphates) of Abū Bakr, Omar and Othmān; and they also talked at length about the reign of Ali b. Abī-Ṭāleb. My father turned to them and said, "You have talked much about [the correlation between] Ali and the caliphate and the caliphate and Ali. Verily, [attaining to the office of] the caliphate was not [a cause for] an adornment of Ali ﷺ; rather, Ali's ﷺ [attaining to the office of] the caliphate was [a cause for] the adornment of that office."⁹³

21. Jāhez Amr b. Bahr (d. 255 AH), the great Mo'tazelite scholar and theologian, says, "It is Ali ﷺ and none other than he who is remembered when there is talk of priority in Islam, [doing battle in] defence of Islam, knowledge of the religion, asceticism and avoidance of the wealth which people team together to accumulate, and talk of munificence and generosity."⁹⁴

22. Jonayd al-Baghdādī (d. 356 AH), the great Sūfī and mystic, was asked about the position of Imam Ali ﷺ in Sūfism. He replied: "If it weren't for the [civil] wars [which rent the community apart and made hatred of Imam Ali ﷺ official policy of the Omayyads], teachings from him concerning the inner sciences would be related [of such power] that they could not be contained in one's breast. He was the master of the true believers (*amīr al-mo'minīn*)."⁹⁵

23. Abol-Faraj al-Esfahānī (d. 356 AH), the great scholar and historian, says of Imam Ali:

    23.1. "The virtues of Ali ﷺ are more than that which can be gathered [in a single volume; in the present work]. Saying too little [about his virtues] has no place in this book (i.e. is below the dignity that this book owes him), and talking at length [about his virtues] takes us far afield of the condition of brevity we set at the outset of the book. We therefore admonish anyone who has not heard much praise of him or for whom the excellence of his virtues has not sunken in. The consensus of opinion of his friends and foe alike maintains that the Commander of the Faithful (Imam Ali ﷺ) has well-known virtues among the populace at large, all of which the experts have not yet put down in writing, but which virtues [this fact notwithstanding] cannot be belittled and covered over: famous virtues which make commentary and elaboration and resorting to various historical reports unnecessary."[96]

23.2. Abol-Faraj al-Esfahānī also states, "Ali ﷺ is the master of the people, is someone who loves God ﷻ and is loved by Him, is the Gate to the City of Knowledge and Wisdom, the narrator [of the real truths of religion] for those who are guided [aright], the light of those who obey [God ﷻ will], and the Patron (*walī*) of those who have [attained to the spiritual station of] God-fearing piety (*taqwā*), and the imam of the righteous (*'ādelīn*). He responded to the call of Islam and attained to faith before anyone else, and his faith and his judgment were steadier and his forbearance and longsuffering (*ḥilm*) greater, and his knowledge more plentiful. He is a model for the pious and the pride (literally, adornment: *zīnā'*) of the worshippers (literally, bondsmen: *'ābedīn*), the revealer (*manbī'*) of the realities of [the Quranic doctrine of] *towḥīd* (the unicity of God ﷻ) and the gauge (*moshīr*) of the luminosity [of the wayfarer on the path] of that science; he is the possessor of a sapiential heart (*qalb al-ūqūl*) and a questioning tongue, and a hearing ear, and he is one who is true to his covenant. He took out the eye of sedition and held adversity at bay and repulsed those who violated their solemn pledges (*al-nākethūn*), and humbled those who abandoned themselves to wrongdoing (*al-qāsetūn*), and repelled those who deviated from the religion (*al-māriqūn*). He was harsh [against the enemies of] God ﷻ religion and was possessed by His Essence."[97]

24. Ebn-e Sīnā (d.428 AH) (or Avicenna as he was known in Medieval Europe), the great philosopher and polymath of the Islamic world, describes Imam Ali ﷺ as follows: "The most noble human being and the most cherished prophet and the Seal of the Messengers ﷺ,

addressing the center of the circle of wisdom and the firmament of reality and the treasury of minds, the Commander of the Faithful Ali ﷺ, stated: 'O Ali ﷺ, when you see the people seeking to gain proximity to their Creator by performing good deeds, surpass them [in virtue] by gaining proximity to Him by the application of your intellect.' These words could not be addressed to anyone but Ali ﷺ, the person whose position among the people is like that of the position of the contemplative sciences [whose subjects are noumena] compared to the empirical sciences [whose subjects are phenomena]. The Prophet ﷺ also told him, 'O Ali ﷺ: expend your efforts in gaining knowledge of the noumenal world (*al-ma'qūlāt*) just as the [generality of] people trouble themselves in a superfluity of their supererogatory acts of ritual worship (*al-ebādāt*); thus will you surpass everyone.' Because Ali ﷺ perceived reality with the eye of the faculty of intellection (*basīrat al-'aql*), phenomena (*mahsūs*) and noumena (*ma'qūl*) were as one to him; and this is why he [was able to] say: "If the veil [of the *dūnya* (the lower or phenomenal world)] were to be lifted, this would not add to the certainty (*yaqīn*) [of my knowledge]."'[98]

25. Abū-Bakr al-Bayhaqī Ahmad b. al-Hosayn (d. 458 AH), the great scholar of the science of hadīth and the author of the celebrated *as-Sonan al-Kobrā* has stated the following concerning Imam Ali : "Ali ﷺ was endowed with every excellence and imbued with every virtue. He was worthy of every [merit of] precedence and [august] rank. No one was more worthy than he of the office of the caliphate during his tenure [of this office].[99] He was in the right when he refrained from seeking the office of the caliphate before his tenure, and he was in the right when he did not give it up during his own tenure."[100]

26. In commenting on the issue of *jahr* (the vocalization of the *bismi'llāh*), Imam Fakhroddīn ar-Rāzī (d. 606 AH), the great Sunnite exegete of the

Quran, mentions the names of a few of the Associates of the Prophet ﷺ who vocalized it (in their ritual devotions) such as Alī b. Abī-Tāleb ؑ, Omar b. al-Khattāb, Abdollāh Eben-Abbās, and Abdollāh Eben-Zobayr, and then gives Imam Ali ؑ a special place among them, stating, "Anyone who defers to Alī b. Abī-Tāleb ؑ in his religion, will be guided [aright] because the Prophet ﷺ stated, 'O God ﷻ! Center *al-haqq* (that which is right and just and true) around Ali ؑ wherever he is! (*allāhomma! ador al-haqq^u ma' 'alī^{un} haytha dār.*)'"[101]

27. Eben Abī'l-Hadīd (d. 656 AH), the great Sunni scholar of the Shāfe'ī rite and the author of a great multi-volume commentary on the *Nahj ol-Balāgha*, is a devotee of Imam Ali's ؑ. In his commentary on the *Nahj ol-Balāgha* he writes about the virtues of the Imam on numerous occasions throughout the book. The sample we present here is from the introduction of his great commentary.

> And as to his virtues, they are at such a high level of greatness, majesty and renown that their mention is beyond [my abilities to convey]… What can I say about someone whose enemies confess to his superiority because they cannot deny his virtues and hide his excellences? It is known that [after] the Omayyads consolidated their power from the east to the west of the [Islamic] territories, they used every possible maneuver in order to put out the light of Imam Ali ؑ, to encourage enmity toward him, and invented faults and falsified slanders against him. They cursed him from every pulpit and would castigate, imprison and even put to death any who dared to eulogize him. They forbade the narration of any hadīth report in which a virtue of Ali's ؑ was mentioned or in which he was mentioned favorably, to the point where the very mention of his name was prohibited. But this did nothing but increase his celebrity; he was like a sachet of musk whose perfume is all the more alluring when it

is out of sight... What can I say about a man to whom every virtue applies and from whom every sect claims descent and with whom every tribe attempts to show their affinity? He is the leader, the fount, the root and the vanguard of every virtue... Among the sciences, it is the religious sciences that he is the archetype and foundation of. Every religious scholar is wholly indebted and beholden to him... And among the [religious] sciences, there is the science of Quranic exegesis and commentary (*tafsīr*), which is derived from him; And among the [religious] sciences, there are the sciences of the *tariqa'* (the narrow path) and *haqīqa'* (the truth; reality) and the [study of the various] states within Sūfism (i.e. the esoteric sciences) in which every great mystic of the Sūfi orders within the world of Islam traces their spiritual lineage back to him, after which point the regression comes to a stop... And among the [religious] sciences, there is the science of Arabic syntax and grammar. Everyone knows that it is he who has created and founded this science and taught its principles and universals to Abū'l-Aswad... But as to courage, he is the man whose [reputation as a warrior] annihilated all trace of the names of every brave warrior who came before him. His reputation in the art of war is so renowned that it will be proverbial until the Resurrection. He was a courageous warrior who never flinched from any battle, never shrank before any legion, and did not engage any enemy in battle without putting an end to him... And his generosity and largess are clear. He would fast and go hungry and give his daily ration to others... And as to jehād for God 🕮 cause: it is as clear as day for friend and foe alike that he is the master of those who fight in God 🕮 cause (*mojāhedūn*); has primacy in jehād been established for any other than he? ... And as to eloquence of rhetoric: he is foremost among the masters of rhetoric; it is said of his speech that it is less that the speech of the Creator but more than the speech of His creatures. People learned rhetoric and eloquence of speech from

Ali ... And as to humbleness, meekness and being good-natured and having a smile on one's face: he was good-natured to the point of being a legend and to where his enemies found fault with him on account of this attribute... And as to asceticism and not being bound to the pleasures of this world: Ali ﷺ was the ascetic par excellence to whom everyone flocked (literally, where camels came to rest). Never once did he eat to the point where his hunger was sated. He would eat the coarsest foods and wear clothes made of the coarsest fabric. And as to his acts of worship: he was the most devout worshipper. He prayed and fasted more than others. People learned how to establish the [supernumerary] night devotions and the invocations of God ﷻ (*dhikr*) and the making a habit of supererogation in their ritual devotions from him. And as to the recitation of the Quran and its reading as a matter of habit: everyone looked to him in these matters. Opinion is unanimous that only Ali ﷺ memorized the Quran during the lifetime of the Prophet ﷺ, and it was he who compiled it... And as to [due] contemplation and wise policy-making: he was endowed with the wisest of thought and had the best policies. It was he who gave council to Omar b. al-Khattāb when the latter was setting out to fight the Byzantines and the Persians, and he also advised Othmān as to what was most expedient for him, which, had Othmān acted according to his wise council, those [divisive] events would not have occurred... And as to his statesmanship: He was a great statesman and harsh when necessary in the way of God ﷻ. He did not consider [his personal relationship to] his cousin when he placed [the burden of] a task on his shoulders, nor that of his brother 'Aqīl when he said some hard words to him [in response to his asking Ali ﷺ to exercise favoritism to his benefit]... What can I say about a person concerning whom the People of the Book (*ahl al-ketāb*)[102] – who deny the prophethood of the Most Noble Prophet ﷺ - are devoted to him, and whose philosophers consider him a great man despite their enmity with the community of Muslims overall, and whose image is drawn by [the artisans of] the Frankish and Byzantine kings and displayed in their shrines and places of worship? ... What can I say about a man whom everyone wants to be associated with so that they can be thought of as pure and good and righteous as a result of such an association? ..."[103]

28. The Egyptian writer Abdorrahmān ash-Sharqāwī (d. 1264 AH) writes the following concerning Imam Ali: "He was the most chivalrous of God's soldiers and the most devoted of them in following the Prophet."[104]

29. The famous Quranic exegete Shaykh Mahmūd al-Ālūsī (d. 1271 AH) writes: "What can one say about those two [Imām Ali and Lady Fātema] other than that Ali was the master (*mowlā*) of all of the true believers (*mo'minīn*) and the successor, executor and heir of the Prophet; and that [Lady] Fātema was a part of Ahmad[105] and a part of Muhammad's being; and that al-Hasan and al-Hosayn were the spirit-edifying breezes of the fragrant flowers of Heaven and the lords of the youth of Heaven. These words are not the words of a Rāfedite; rather, anyone who believes in anything other than this is utterly lost."[106]

30. In his commentary on the *Nahj ol-Balagha*, the Egyptian Moftī Shaykh Muhammad Abdo (d. 1323 AH) states: "Among the men of Arabic letters, everyone admits that Alī b. Abī-Tāleb had the most noble and most eloquent speech, and was endowed with the greatest vocabulary, the highest points of style and the most comprehensive and valuable meaning after the word of God and of His Prophet."[107]

31. Shebli Shamīl (d. 1335 AH), the Lebanese writer, writes: "Alī b. Abī-Tāleb ﷺ is the greatest of the greats. He is the only example of one who has not been equalled in either East or West, be it in the past or the present."[108]

32. Khalil Gibran, the renowned Christian Arab poet (d. 1349 AH) says, "Truly, Ali ﷺ is one of the greats of all times and of all places, intellectually, spiritually, and in the power of his oratory."[109]

33. The famous Egyptian writer, Abbās Mahmūd Aqqād (d. 1383 AH) says, "It has been said in truth that given his unique legendary characteristics, Ali ﷺ was a pure Muslim. Without a doubt, none has appeared in the new religion with Ali's sincerity and depth in Islam. He was a true Muslim in his ritual devotions, his knowledge, in his heart, and in his intellect... He was devoted to the worship and devotion of God ﷻ; it was as if the ritual acts of devotion were as play for him which brought him inner peace, and not an obligation which had been mandated for him... In his knowledge and understanding of the religious sciences, he had the most beautiful Islam, just as was the case in his devotions and acts. His authoritative religio-legal opinions (*fatāwā*, sing. *fatwā*) were the sources of emulation for the caliphs and the Associates during the caliphates of Abu Bakr, Omar and Othmān. Very rarely can one find a religio-juridical issue for which Ali has provided a ruling with the best possible reasons provided and which is still acted upon to this day."[110]

34. Tāhā Hosayn, the famous Egyptian writer (d. 1393 AH) writes, "Omar – may God ﷻ have mercy on his soul – recognized Ali's ﷺ knowledge and understanding of the religious sciences, and every time the state ran into difficulties, he would seek Ali's ﷺ help; and when he appointed the Council of Six [to determine his successor], he told them, 'If the helm of the ship of state is given to he whose hair has fallen on both sides of his

head [reference to Imam Ali ﷺ], he will take them on the right path.' He did so while mentioning Ali's countless excellences and virtues – virtues which all of the Associates of the Prophet ﷺ with all their differences, and all of the righteous from the *tābe'īn* (followers) generation, were well acquainted with, and in which Sunnis believe, just as his Shī'a (followers) believe in them."[111]

34.1. Concerning the way in which Imam Ali dealt with the issues of the caliphate of Othmān, TāHā Hosayn says, "Imam Ali ﷺ found himself confronted with these momentous events and in the best situation in the center of this dark and twisted disturbance: a sincere faith in God ﷺ, wanting what is best for Islam, insurrection for that which is right, and steadfastness in maintaining the Straight Path, in which no deviation is tolerated and in which there is not the slightest shortcoming. He only saw the truth and went toward it and did not turn away from it and did not couple it to a favorable end for himself. It made no difference to him whether the end of the road entailed victory or defeat for himself, or life or death. What was important for him was that he attained a clear conscience for himself and God ﷺ good pleasure during the journey."[112]

34.2. Professor Hasan Ebrāhīm Hasan, a contemporary scholar and the president of Assiut University and a visiting professor at the universities of Cairo, Baghdad and others in the United States states, "Ali b. Abī-Tāleb ﷺ was endowed with admirable qualities. He was raised in the Prophet's ﷺ household and trained in the lofty ways of courtesy (*adab*) and in the noble code of moral conduct of that eminent personality ﷺ. He was the first person to enter into Islam. The Prophet ﷺ had him by his side and placed him in a fitting station and willed to him [authority] concerning many of the affairs [of the community]. Ali ﷺ passed these tests well, aided Islam sincerely, and gained renown for his gallantry and courage… as he did for his chivalry, trustworthiness, respect for his covenants, and diligence in guarding the public treasury... He would be consulted in many of the difficult issues concerning the proper execution of the religion, inheritance laws, and difficult judgements. It has been related that Omar, the second caliph, sook refuge in God ﷻ for any difficulty in which he did not have Ali ؑ by his side... He was a legend in the art of oratory; he would speak and win over people's hearts; he would deliver a sermon and agitate people's souls and muster together an army ready to do battle... He was full of verve, intelligent, far-sighted, victorious in battle, a wise councilor, sagacious, trustworthy, and acted with nobility toward his enemies. And it is for these reasons that his sermons and verses are renowned throughout the Islamic world."[113]

35. Muhammad Reḍā, another contemporary Egyptian writer, states: "Alī b. Abī-Tāleb ؑ was raised and trained in the household of prophethood. He entered into Islam before anyone else and grew up within it, while his spirit was imbibed and quenched with the teachings of the Prophet ﷺ [in person]. He spent his youth doing good all the while witnessing revelation descending unto the Prophet ﷺ. He was a scribe of revelation, but no report has reached us that tells us when, under what conditions, and under whose tutelage he learned how to read and write... He kept the company of the Prophet ﷺ. He knew the Quran by heart, related hadīth reports of the Prophet ﷺ, and had a deep understanding of Islam. Courage was a part of his nature... He spent the best years of his early life in defense of the Messenger ﷺ of God ﷻ without feeling the least bit of fear, and he spent the rest of his life spreading the message of Islam, defending its standard and ensuring its survival. When we read about the battles fought by the Prophet ﷺ, we see Ali's ؑ name in its chronicles, sometimes as the standard-bearer in the field of battle, and at times breaking the front lines of the enemy or bringing order to the army of the believers. We see him fighting the great warriors of the Qūraysh, who

were the enemies of Islam, and defeating them; and we see him conquering the fortresses of the enemy, and destroying the false idols of the polytheists."¹¹⁴

36. Mikhail Na'īma, a famous contemporary Lebanese writer, writes, "The celebrity of the Imam ﷺ is never limited to the field of battle; rather, he was a champion in the spotlessness of his vision, the purity of his conscience, in his mesmerizing eloquence, the warmth of his faith, the magnitude of his serenity, his charity to the dispossessed and downtrodden, and in his taking the side of the righteous wherever there was a call for it. His championship is of such a magnitude that we can return to it again and again, today and every day and continue to learn from it.

37. George Jordac, the Orthodox Christian Lebanese writer who was a devotee of Imam Ali ﷺ and has written several books about him¹¹⁵ writes, "O world! How would it be if you would gather all your strength and, in each era, produce an Ali with his intellect, heart and tongue?"¹¹⁶

38. The contemporary biographer Khayrod-Dīn Zarkalī (d. 1410 AH) writes, "[Imam Ali ﷺ was] one of the courageous warriors, a great orator, juridical savant. After Khadīja, he was the first person to enter into Islam. He was born in Mecca and was raised in the lap of the Prophet ﷺ, and never separated from him. He was the standard-bearer for most of the battles fought by the community of faith. At the time when the Prophet ﷺ made bonds of brotherhood between the Emigrants and Helpers, he told Ali ﷺ, 'You are my brother.'"¹¹⁷

2. Imam Hasan b. Ali

Imam Hasan b. Ali ﷺ who was the grandson of the Prophet ﷺ and the second Imam of the Shī'a, is held in high regard in the Sunni community, who consider him and his younger brother Imam Hosayn ﷺ to be the "Lords of the youth of Paradise" according to reliable reports[118] related from the Prophet ﷺ. Some Sunni scholars, as well as non-Muslim writers, have written books about Imam Hasan ﷺ, such as *Al-Hasan the son of Ali* by Towfīq Abū-l'Elm, *Al-Hasan and al-Hosayn, Grandsons of the Messenger of God* by Muhammad ar-Reḍā, and *The Life of Imam al-Hasan* by Mahmūd ash-Sheblī, and The Imam al-Hasan: the Squandered Fount by Soleymān al-Kattānī, a Christian author.

Some of what the Associates of the Prophet ﷺ, the Followers (*at-tābe'īn*), and scholars of the Sunni community have said about Imam al-Hasan ﷺ are as follows:

1. One day 'Amr b. al-Āṣ (d. 43 AH), Mo'āwiya's friend and wily vizier, saw Imam Hasan ﷺ approaching him. He pointed at him and said, "This man is the most beloved denizen of the earth to those who are in the Heavens."[119] This same statement has also been narrated by Abdollāh b. 'Amr b. al-Āṣ (d. 65 AH).[120]

2. When Imam Hasan ﷺ attained to martyrdom, the Omayyad caliph Marwān b. Hakam (d. 65 AH) wept at his funeral. Imam Hosayn ﷺ said to him, "Do you then weep for his loss even though you afflicted him with [unbearable] sadness?" Pointing at a mountain, Marwān said, "I did so to a person who had more forbearance than this mountain."[121]

3. Abdollāh b. Zobayr (d. 73 AH) became a pretender to the caliphate in the year 63 AH and gained control of a large swath of the territory of the

Hejāz. They asked him who most closely resembles the Prophet ﷺ. He said, al-Hasan b. Ali ؑ most closely resembled the Prophet ﷺ and was the person dearest to his heart."[122]

3.1. Abdollāh b. Zobayr was asked about Imam Hasan ؑ. He said, "He is the son of [Lady] Fātema ؑ. I swear [upon my oath] to God ﷻ! Women have not given birth [to anyone] like [unto those to whom] she has."[123]

4. Anas b. Mālek (d. 93 AH), an Associate and manservant of the Prophet ﷺ says, "No one resembled the Prophet ﷺ more than al-Hasan b. Ali ؑ."[124]

5. ʿAmīr b. Eshāq, a narrator of hadīth reports from the generation of the Followers, says, "No one has been like al-Hasan b. Ali ؑ in that when he talked to me, I wanted him to continue talking and not to stop."[125]

6. The biographer Eben Abdol-Berr (d. 463 AH) states, "Imam Hasan ؑ was forbearing, pious and virtuous. His piety and virtue beckoned him to abandon [the pleasures of] this world and rulership in the way of seeking God ﷻ good pleasure."[126]

7. The historian Eben Asāker (d. 571 AH) introduces him as follows: "Abū Muhammad al-Hasan b. Alī b. Abī-Tāleb b. Abdol-Mottaleb b. Hāshem b. ʿAbd-Manāf b. Qasī Abū Muhammad al-Hāshemī ؑ, is the grandson of the Prophet ﷺ and his fragrant flower and one of the masters of the youth of paradise."[127]

8. The great biographer, prosopographer and historian Shamsoddīn adh-Dhahabī (d. 748 AH) says, "The virtues of Imam Hasan ؑ, may God ﷻ be pleased with him, are many. He was a dignitary [of the Muslim community], endowed with forbearance and serenity, dignity and honor.

He detested the seditions and the sword, and was munificent and the subject of profuse praise."[128]

8.1. Dhahabī also states: "al-Hasan b. Alī b. Abī-Tāleb b. Abdol-Mottaleb b. Hāshem ﷺ was an imam (leader), a dignitary [of the Muslim community], the flagrant flower of the Prophet ﷺ, his grandson and one of the masters of the youth of paradise."[129]

8.2. And again: "This leader was a dignitary [of the Muslim community], was righteous, handsome, wise, munificent, the subject of praise, pious, God-fearing, dignified and honorable."[130]

9. The biographer Salāhoddīn as-Safdī (d. 764 AH) states: "Imam Hasan ﷺ lived just as the Prophet ﷺ had described: he was dedicated to the ritual devotions and prayer, he was knowledgeable in the religion, he was gracious, virtuous, honorable, noble, forbearing, and eloquent. He made the Major Pilgrimage (*hajj*) on foot twenty-five times [from Medina], even though there were camels available [in his caravan]. In seeking God ﷻ good pleasure, He gave away all of his wealth to the needy on three different occasions, to the extent that he gave away his shoes and kept only his slippers for himself."[131]

10. The great biographer and Quranic exegete Eben Kathīr (d. 774 AH) states: "Imam Hasan was the master of the Muslim [community] and a scholar among the Associates of the Prophet ﷺ. The proof that he is [i.e. should be considered as] one of the Rāshedūn (Rightly-Guided) Caliphs is the hadīth report of the Prophet who is reported to have said, "The caliphate after me is [i.e. will last for] thirty years."[132]

11. Allāme Eben Sabbāgh al-Makkī (d. 855 AH), the leader of the Mālekī religio-legal rite (*madhhab*) of his era, writes about Imam Hasan ﷺ as follows: "His dedication to the ritual devotions, to supplication and to the ascetic life is well known… Dignity and generosity are two instincts

which are planted like a tree in him, and his continual giving to freed slaves was a practice of his on which he always acted. He talked like his father, and his position in the art of rhetoric was such that he was second to none."[133]

12. Tāhā Hosayn, the famous Egyptian writer (d. 1393 AH) writes, "He had a gentle spirit, he was well-spoken, erudite and cultured; he was friendly and popular among the people. The youth among the Quraysh and the Helpers (ansār) liked him on account of these qualities, and the elders and statesmen of the Associates of the Prophet ﷺ liked him for these reasons as well as because of his standing in the eyes of the Prophet ﷺ, and the general populace liked him on account of these attributes as well as for his generosity and largess towards the needy, [which was ever present] whether they asked for his help or not."[134]

13. The contemporary biographer Khayroddīn Zarkalī (d. 1410 AH) writes, "[Imam Hasan was] wise, forbearing, righteous, eloquent, was the greatest of orators and [was peerless] in the art of improvised speech. He made the Major Pilgrimage (hajj) twenty times on foot [from Medina to Mecca and back]."[135]

14. Muhammad Reḍā, another contemporary Egyptian writer, states: "Imam Hasan ﷺ was forbearing, generous, pious, possessed of dignity, honor and a serenity of spirit, munificent, well-praised, peace-loving, and hated the seditions and the shedding of blood."[136]

3. Imam Hosayn b. Ali

The personality of Imam Hosayn ﷺ and his insurrection and martyrdom in Karbalā is greatly respected and valued among a great number of people within the Sunni community, and beyond that, among all those who pine for justice and freedom from oppression from all nations and religions around the world. Many books have been written about the Imam ﷺ.[137] Some Sunni and non-Muslim writers and scholars have written voluminous books about him.

From the time of the martyrdom of Imam Hosayn ﷺ to today, hundreds of poets have written elegies and requiems in many languages about the greatness of the character of the Imam ﷺ and about the heart-rending events that took place in Karbalā on that fateful day of Āshūrā (on the 10th of the Month of Moharram of the year 61 AH/ October 10th, 680 AD) when Imam Hosayn ﷺ and his family and companions were massacred by the forces of the Omayyad dynasty. A large number of these poets are from the Sunni community. Among these poets, the names of great poets can also be seen."[138]

The following is a selection of some of what the Associates of the Prophet ﷺ, the generation of the Followers, and Sunni scholarship has said about Imam Hosayn ﷺ.

1. One day 'Amr b. al-Ās (d. 43 AH), Mo'āwiya's vizier and an enemy of the *Ahl al-Bayt* (the House of the Prophet ﷺ) saw Imam Hosayn ﷺ approaching. He pointed to him and said, "This man is the most beloved denizen of the earth to those who are in the Heavens."[139] This same statement has also been narrated by Abdollāh b. 'Amr b. al-Ās (d. 65 AH)[140]; as well as by Abdollāh b. Omar (d. 73 AH), the son of the second caliph.[141]

2. Abū-Horeyra (d. 59 AH), an Associate of the Prophet ﷺ, addressing Imam Hosayn ﷺ, has said, "If the people knew what I know about you, they would carry you on their shoulders."[142]

3. One day Jāber b. Abdollāh al-Ansārī (d. 59 AH), the great Associate of the Prophet ﷺ, saw Imam Hosayn ﷺ entering the mosque. He pointed to him and said, "Anyone who desires to gaze upon the Master of the Youth of Heaven, let him look at this man."[143]

4. The great biographer, prosopographer and historian Shamsoddīn adh-Dhahabī (d. 748 AH) says the following concerning Imam Hosayn ﷺ: "Hosayn ﷺ was a martyr, a leader who was noble and who had attained to perfection, the grandson and beloved of the Prophet ﷺ, and his fragrant flower in this world."[144]

5. Allāme Eben Sabbāgh al-Makkī (d. 855 AH), the leader of the Mālekī religio-legal rite (*madhhab*) of his era, says the following concerning Imam Hosayn ﷺ: "al-Hosayn's ﷺ place in this noble family is in its most lofty heights, heights where [even] the stars of the Heavens dare not tread. He attained to [an understanding of] the most demanding teachings with the purity of his soul whereupon [exceptional] realities were unveiled to him. The fame of his virtues reached everywhere and to the ears of friends and foe alike. When the most demanding trophies of greatness and glory were being divvied out, he attained to the fertile lands of glory. Virtues are gathered in the person of [Imam] Hosayn ﷺ and his brother, among which there is not a single difference. And why, pray, should this not be the case when those two were the children of [Imam] Ali ﷺ and [Lady] Fātema ﷺ, and are the grandchildren of one who is the Lord of the Messengers and the Seal of Prophethood ﷺ? [Imam] Hosayn ﷺ is a person who sharpened the sword and spear and went to battle with malicious warriors."[145]

6. The famous Egyptian writer, Abbās Mahmūd Aqqād (d. 1383 AH) says the following about Imam Hosayn ﷺ, "He mastered the highest knowledge, the Islamic mode of courteous conduct (*adab*), and the

martial arts that were taught to the children of that era. A large number of the Sūfī [orders] and divines have taken the teachings that they rely on and refer to through him and up to [his father] Alī b. Abī-Tāleb ﷺ, [who is their ultimate source]. The Angel of Eloquence had been bestowed unto him such that his rhetoric was resonant, alluring and penetrating... He left posterity the noble mode of courteous conduct worthy of the honorable household in which he was raised... Uncommon tales have been related concerning his mastery of the religious sciences and the art of letters being tested, just as similarly fascinating accounts have reached us about the mastery of his father. He was the subject of frequent visits by poets on account of his mastery of the art of rhetoric and his celebrity as an orator, and their hunger for hearing his speech exceeded their appetite for his largess and munificence. Besides his generosity, he was known for his courage and fidelity, two of the highest human character traits which were worthy of his august house... The enormity of [Imam] Hosayn's ﷺ courage is not something that should surprise us because he acquired it from the motherlode of its mine. Courage is a virtue which fathers leave as an inheritance and which sons inherit... No human being has had the courage which was demonstrated by [Imam] Hosayn ﷺ in Karbalā."[146]

7. Omar Farrūkh, the contemporary Lebanese writer and translator, says: "Today we Muslims (in all our lands) are in need of a Hosayn ﷺ to guide us to the right path and to teach us how to stand up for justice.... Who else other than [Imam] Hosayn can one point to (who is yet alive) in our own time who is endowed with a soundness of moral character such that they rise up and lead an insurrection for establishing justice and for extinguishing the reign of profane ideologies?"[147]

8. The contemporary author Ali b. Muhammad b. Abdollāh al-Fekrī says of Imam Hosayn ﷺ that "he was the best man of his era the like of whom was unknown either in the east or the west of the world."[148]

9. In a commentary on the book *Hosayn ﷺ the son of Ali ﷺ, an offshoot of the Prophet*, Dr. Muhammad b. Fathollāh al-Badrān states: "The pure Master, the Imam Abū Abdollāh al-Hosayn ﷺ was the son of the daughter of the Prophet ﷺ and his fragrant flower and the son of the Commander of the Faithful, Ali ﷺ; as such, he was a protégé of the House of Prophethood and was endowed with the most noble lineage and the most perfected spirit. The most excellent virtues and proper conduct were gathered in his person, virtues such as the greatness of spiritual will (*hemma'*), the pinnacle of courage, the highest rank of munificence, mastery of the mysteries of the sciences, eloquence of speech, standing up against injustice, enjoining the doing of that which is right and forbidding the doing of that which is wrong, honorable humility, soundness of character, forbearance, modesty, spiritual chivalry and piety. He had a wholesome and innate disposition (*fetra'*), a beautiful mind and a strong build. In addition to all of these virtues, we must add a superfluity of ritual devotions and prayer, and good deeds such as fasting, making the major and minor pilgrimages to the Ka'ba, *jehād* in God ﷻ cause, and beneficence."[149]

10. The contemporary author Foād Ali Reḍā says the following about Imam Hosayn ﷺ: "The last word belongs to the virtues of my master and the one who is responsible for all my blessings; the pure one, and the grandson who is endowed with all of the virtues and with the height of proper conduct, generosity, courage, martyrdom, forbearance, scholarship, my Lord and Master Abī-Abdollāh al-Hosayn ﷺ. He is the leader of the devotees, the qibla (direction of prayer) of the *tālebān* (those who seek [ever closer proximity to God ﷻ]), the station of contentment

and acceptance, the master of the People of Beautiful Righteous Conduct in Heaven, the key to the paths of the needful of God ❧ loving kindness, and the most beloved of the People of the Earth in the heart of Muhammad ﷺ, the Master of the Prophets."[150]

11. Muhammad Reḍā, another contemporary Arab author writes the following about Imam Hosayn ﷺ: "He fasted often and spend long hours in devotion and supplication, and had many virtues. He was munificent and gave largely in charity and performed good deeds."[151]

12. Dr. Zāhīya Dajjānī writes the following about Imam Hosayn ﷺ: "[Imam] Hosayn ﷺ, who was greatly influenced by his father's teachings... sought to find his calling in life by understanding the reality of things so that his faith was formed on the basis of wholesome ideas and a brilliant mind. Beside this, he had trained his conscience to be completely subservient to [the will of] God ❧. He soared with his emotions and took off with his intellect. With a steady will and a strong desire for seeing justice prevail, he sought to establish his justice. He established the principles of his life on the pillars of justice, and was prepared to give his life and wealth in the way of establishing justice without any fear whatsoever of death, and thus attained to martyrdom. This is how he became the most prominent legend of abnegation and self-sacrifice in history, and how he left an undying legacy behind."[152]

13. Cardinal Doctor Bartholomaus Ajamī says, "From the Christian perspective, [Imam] Hosayn ﷺ is a martyr, just as he is a martyr from the perspective of Islam and other religions, because he sacrificed himself for the cause of attaining to all of the ideals that are included in the humanities and whose benefits are not limited to any given individual."[153]

14. Professor Abdollāh Shaytī says, "[Imam] Hosayn ﷺ and his insurrection have continually been a source of inspiration to free-thinkers and visionaries throughout history, who find an endless treasure of ethical conduct in the way in which the Prince of the Martyrs ﷺ lived and died."[154]

15. The Iraqi poet Ahmad Matar says, "Does an analogue exist within the prophets and martyrs [in all of history] of the abnegation and self-sacrifice of Hosayn ﷺ the Martyr, the father and master of all martyrs? Can one at all find in all of the religions of the world past and present an example of the altruism and selflessness of the grandson of the Prophet ﷺ of Islam who said of him, 'Hosayn ﷺ is [a part] of me, and I am [a part] of Hosayn ﷺ'?"[155]

16. The Christian writer Antoine Bara has written a book called *Hosayn in Christian Thought* in which he analyses the personality and insurrection of Imam Hosayn ﷺ. At the end of his book, he says, "Hosayn ﷺ is the Lord of the Martyrs in the fields of the battle for justice. He is a person whose insurrection is the practical application of the inner voice of all of the divine religions throughout the course of history... [Imam] Hosayn ﷺ is the essence of every religion throughout every era. He is the unique witness to the deception of hiding truth and justice in the body of being; but God ﷻ will not stand this, and will perfect His light. God ﷻ wisdom shall not be content until his goal is realized in all its majesty and glory, so that all of the horizons of humanity are covered with purity and justice and virtue. Hosayn ﷺ is the guiding flame and the lantern of purity and the exemplary model by which these goals are attained, and by the right of the essence of every religion, will so remain until the Day of Resurrection."[156]

17. Mahmūd Shablī, the contemporary Arab author, has a book entitled *The Life of Imam Hosayn* ﷺ. In one of its sections of it he talks about the name of the Imam :

> "His grandfather named him Hosayn ﷺ. What indications are latent in this name? The person who named him [53:3] *does not speak out of his own desires*. It is perhaps a diminutive form of the word *hosn* (excellence, goodness, virtue). It seems the diminution refers to the placement of all excellences and virtues in the person of Imam Hosayn ﷺ. He is a single person, but his *hosn* is equivalent to a nation (*omma'*) in which all virtues are present. The peak of every goodness has somehow been fitted into him. He is Hosayn ﷺ who, from the moment of his birth to the moment of his death, was as such."[157]

18. In his introduction to Abdolrahmān ash-Sharqāwī's book *The Martyred Insurgent*, Dr. Sāleh 'Adīma states, "How was it possible for them so lightly to give themselves the permission to kill the unstained grandson of the Prophet ﷺ? One who was the apple of the Prophet's ﷺ eyes, and the closest of people to him in terms both of his appearance and his conduct. He was an [entire] nation of knowledge, forbearance, purity and piety who had epiphanized in a single being."[158]

4. Imam Ali b. Hosayn Zeyn ol-Ābedīn

Imam Ali b. al-Hosayn ﷺ is known as Zeynol-Abedīn (the Adornment of the Bondsmen or Devotees [of God ﷻ]) in Sunnite sources, and mention of him under this title can be found in abundance. Sunni scholars and some non-Muslim scholars have written several books about him.

The Shī'a Imāms in the Words of Sunni Scholarship

The following is a selection of some of what the Associates of the Prophet ﷺ, the generation of the Followers, and Sunni scholarship has said about Imam Zeynol-Ābedīn ﷺ.

1. Saī'd b. Mosayyab (d. 94 AH) who is one of the *tābe'īn* (Followers) and one of the great scholars of the Quranic sciences of Medina has said, "I have not seen anyone who has [attained to] the heights of [the spiritual station of] God-fearing piety (*taqwā*) as has Ali b. al-Hosayn Zeynol-Ābedīn ﷺ."[159]

2. A report is related about Omar b. Abdol-Azīz (d. 101 AH), the caliph of the Banī-Omayya (the Omayyads) who is highly respected by the Sunni, that one day, he was in a gathering wherein Ali b. al-Hosayn Zeyn ol-Ābedīn ﷺ was seated and had just gotten up to leave. Addressing those present, Omar b. Abdol-Azīz asked, "Who is the most noble of people?" He was told, "You (the Banī-Omayya) are the most noble of people; because during the Days of Ignorance (*jāhelia'* – the days before the advent of the Prophet's mission), you were of the nobility, and in the era of Islam too, the caliphate is yours." Omar b. Abdol-Azīz said, "Never! The most noble of men is this man who has just risen from our midst; because the most noble of men is he whom everyone desires to be like, and who does not desire to be like anyone else, and Ali b. al-Hosayn ﷺ is that person."[160]

3. Muhammad b. Muslim az-Zahrī (d. 124 AH) who was an Associate of the Prophet ﷺ and a student of Imam Zeyn ol-Ābedīn's ﷺ, is one of the great magisters (foqahā; religio-legal scholars) within the Sunnite tradition, and was the first person among them to systematically compile hadīth reports.[161] Many reports have reached us from him which are in praise of the Imam , including:

3.1. "I have not seen anyone as preeminent as Ali b. al-Hosayn ﷺ among the Banī-Hāshem (the clan of the Prophet ﷺ)."[162]

3.2. "I have not seen anyone as preeminent as Ali b. al-Hosayn ﷺ among the Qūraysh (the greater tribe of the Prophet ﷺ)."[163]

3.3. "I have not seen anyone as learned in the religious sciences as Ali b. al-Hosayn ﷺ."[164]

3.4. "Ali b. al-Hosayn ﷺ was the most preeminent man of his House and the one who was the most obedient to God ﷻ [will]."[165]

3.5. "I am more beholden to Ali b. al-Hosayn ﷺ than to anyone else."[166]

4. Zeyd b. Muslim (d. 136 AH), an early magister and Quranic exegete from Medina says, "I have not kept the company of anyone from among the People of the Qibla (i.e. among Muslims) [as exceptional] as Ali b. al-Hosayn ﷺ."[167]

5. Abū-Hāzem b. Salmaᵗ b. Diyār (d. 140 AH), the great religious scholar and judge of Medina says, "I have not seen anyone as learned in the religious sciences as Ali b. al-Hosayn ﷺ."[168]

6. Yahyā b. Sa'īd (d. 143 AH), another great religious scholar and judge of Medina says, "I have heard hadīth reports from Ali b. al-Hosayn ﷺ and he is the most preeminent among the Banī-Hāshem. He used to establish a thousand cycles (rak'aʿ) of the ritual devotions in [a single] day and night [cycle]."[169]

7. Mālek b. Anas (d. 179 AH), the eponymous founder of the Mālekī religio-legal rite (madhhab), states, "Ali b. al-Hosayn ﷺ set out for pilgrimage in a state of ritual consecration (ehrām), and when he was in the stage of pronouncing the labbayk ("I am at thy command, [my Lord]."), he passed out, such that he fell off his camel and was injured. I am told that he used to establish a thousand cycles (rak'aʿ) of the ritual

devotions in [a single] day and night [cycle] until the day he died.[170] He was given the title "Zeyn ol-Abedī" (the Adornment of the Bondsmen [of God ﷻ]) because of the intensity of his devotions."[171] Mālek b. Anas also states, "There was no one as preeminent as Ali b. al-Hosayn ﷺ among the House (*ahl al-bayt* ﷺ) of the Prophet ﷺ)."[172]

8. Imam Muhammad b. Edrīs ash-Shāfeʾī (d. 204 AH), the eponymous founder of the Shāfeʾī religio-legal rite (*madhhab*), states, "Ali b. al-Hosayn ﷺ who was the most learned person in the religious sciences in the city of Medina used to rely on *akhbār ol-āhād* (i.e. hadīth reports with only a single chain of narrators in its provenance title or *sanad*)."[173]

9. Muhammad b. Omar al-Wāqedī (d. 207 AH), one of the earliest historians and biographers, says, "Ali b. al-Hosayn ﷺ was one of the most devout and pious and God-fearing of people."[174]

10. Eben Saʾd (d. 230 AH) and Eben Asāker (d. 571 AH), two great Sunnite historians, say the same thing about the Imam: "Ali b. al-Hosayn ﷺ was [a] reliable [transmitter of hadīth], trustworthy, *kathīr ol-hadīth* (i.e. transmitted many hadīth reports), was preeminent, and pious."[175]

11. Muhammad b. Yazīd al-Mobarrad (d. 286 AH), the leader of the Basran grammarians against the Kufan school, states, "It is related that Ali b. al-Hosayn ﷺ was the best and most God-fearing of people."[176]

12. Abū-Bakr Ahmad b. Abdollāh al-Barqī (d. 270 AH), the scholar of prosopography, says, "Ali b. al-Hosayn ﷺ was the most preeminent man of his era."[177]

13. The celebrated historian al-Yaʾqūbī (d. 284 AH) says, "Ali b. al-Hosayn ﷺ was the most preeminent man and was given over to devotions and

supplication more than the other men [of his generation (?)]. He was referred to as Zeyn ol-Ābedīn ﷺ; but also as *dhī ath-thafanāt* or the owner of calluses, because the marks of many hours spent in prostration were evident on him. He used to make one thousand cycles of the ritual devotions a day. When the ritual washing of the body of the deceased (*ghosl*) was performed on him after his death, sore marks were seen on his shoulders like the marks on the back of a camel. When his family was asked what they were the traces of, they said, 'These are as a result of carrying food at night to the houses of the indigent.'"[178]

14. Abū-Hātam Muhammad b. Hebbān (d. 354 AH) the great historian and prosopographer says, "Ali b. al-Hosayn b. Ali b. Abī-Tāleb ﷺ was a scholar of religion of the House of the Prophet ﷺ, and one of the most preeminent men of the Banī-Hāshem and of Medina."[179]

15. The great biographer Hāfez Abū-No'aym al-Isfahānī (d. 430 AH) says, "Ali b. al-Hosayn b. Ali b. Abī-Tāleb ﷺ, may God ﷻ be pleased with them, was the adornment of the worshipers, the loadstar (*manār*) of the devoutly obedient (*qānetīn*), true, munificent and kind."[180]

16. Muhammad b. Talha ash-Shāfe'ī (d. 652 AH) says, "Ali b. al-Hosayn b. Ali b. Abī-Tāleb ﷺ was the adornment of the worshipers, the exemplary model of the ascetics, the Lord and Master of the God-fearing, and the leader of the true believers. His conduct testifies that he was of the lineage of the Prophet ﷺ. His visage proves his proximity to God ﷻ. His callouses tell the tale of his profuse devotions and night prayers. His foregoing the petty benefits of the world speaks to his asceticism… He was gifted with "impossible wonders" and extra-ordinary feats (*karāmāt*) which are visible for those who have the sight to see and are proven with *motewāter*[181] hadīth; and everyone is agreed that he is a king in [the world of] the hereafter.

17. Eben Abī'l-Hadīd (d. 656 AH), the exegete of the *Nahj ol-Balāgha* writes, "We have three personalities who are cousins. All three are called Ali, and all three were worthy of the caliphate on account of the breadth of their knowledge of religious jurisprudence (*fiqh*), their piety, intellectual acumen, experience and the esteem in which they were held by the general populace. They are: Ali b. Hosayn b. Ali ﷺ, Ali b. Abdollāh b. Abbās, and Ali b. Abdollāh b. Ja'far. All of them were flawless, perfected [men], preeminent over others [of their generation], and endowed with every possible virtue."[182]

18. Shaykh ol-Islām Eben Teymīya (d. 748 AH) says, "Ali b. al-Hosayn ﷺ was one of the great men among the Followers (*tābe'īn*), and their Lord and Master in knowledge and religion."[183]

19. The great biographer, prosopography and historian Shamsoddīn adh-Dhahabī (d. 748 AH) says, "Ali b. Hosayn b. Ali b. Abī-Tāleb b. Abdol-Mottaleb b. Hāshem b. 'Abd-Manāf b. Qasī, as-Seyyed al-Imām Zeyn ol-Ābedīn ﷺ ... He has an incredible majesty, and I swear [upon my oath] to God ﷻ! He was worthy of such majesty. He was worthy of the office of the great leadership (*imāmat al-ozmā*) on account of his nobility, prominence, knowledge, proximity to God ﷻ, and the perfection of his intellect."[184]

20. The great Quranic exegete Eben Kathīr states, "The scholars of the House of the Prophet ﷺ are among the people who, when they are on the right path, are among the foremost scholars, such as Ali ﷺ and Eben Abbas, and Ali's two sons: al-Hasan ﷺ and al-Hosayn ﷺ, and Muhammad b. al-Hanfīya, and Ali b. al-Hosayn Zeyn ol-Ābedīn ﷺ, and Ali b. Abdollāh b. Abbās, and Abū-Ja'far al-Bāqer ﷺ, i.e. Muhammad b. Ali b. Hosayn, and his son, Ja'far ﷺ, and their like,

people who have held fast to the Firm Handle of the Divine and were aware of every person's proper place."[185]

21. Allāme Muhammad b. Ahmad b. Abdol-Hādī al-Hanbalī (d. 756 AH) says, "Ali b. Hosayn Zeyn ol-Ābedīn ﷺ was one of the great men among the Followers (tābe'īn) in knowledge and religion."[186]

22. Allāme Eben Sabbāgh al-Makkī (d. 855 AH), the leader of the Mālekī religio-legal rite (madhhab) of his era, writes about Imam Zeyn ol-Ābedīn ﷺ as follows: "Among the children of Hosayn b. Ali ﷺ, only the name of Imam Zeyn ol-Ābedīn ﷺ became immortal and is the subject of abundant praise… In remembrance of Imam Zeyn ol-Ābedīn ﷺ who was the fourth Imam, there are "impossible wonders" and extraordinary feats (karāmāt) which are visible for those with sight to see and are proven with motewāter[187] hadīth… His virtues are abundant, and the excellence of his character traits are famous among the people."[188]

23. Muhammad Khāje-ye Pārsā-ye Bokhārī (d. 865 AH), the magister (faqīh), scholar of the science of hadīth, and Sūfī, says, "Ali b. Hosayn Zeyn ol-Ābedīn ﷺ was [a] reliable [transmitter of hadīth], trustworthy, kathīr ol-hadīth (i.e. transmitted many hadīth reports), preeminent, and the scholars are unanimous in [acclaiming] his majesty in everything."[189]

24. Hāfez Zeyneddīn Zakarīā b. Muhammad al-Ansārī al-Sanakī al-Azharī ash-Shāfe'ī (d. 925 AH) says, "Ali b. Hosayn b. Ali b. Abī-Tāleb Zeyn ol-Ābedīn ﷺ … [and two other people] had surpassed the other scholars of religion in Medina in their piety and God-wariness. Ali b. Hosayn ﷺ was given the title "Zeyn ol-Abedīn" (the Adornment of the Bondsmen [of God ﷻ]) because of the extent of his ritual devotions and supplications. He used to establish a thousand cycles (rak'a') of the ritual devotions in [a single] day and night [cycle] until the day he died. In his

book ad-Dorr on-Nafis, my great grandfather says that Ali b. Hosayn b. Alī b. Abī-Tāleb Zeyn ol-Ābedīn ﷺ was one of the greatest devotees of prayer and supplication and was of the Prophet's ﷺ lineage from the generation of the Followers. He had attained to great ranks in certainty (*yaqīn*) and the station of being exclusively occupied with wayfaring toward God ﷻ (*enqeta'*) and [being dedicated to] following the Prophet ﷺ. The caliph Abdol-Mālek b. Marwān thought very highly of him and honored him."[190]

25. Shamsoddīn Muhammad b. Tūtūn (Eben Batūta) al-Hanafī (d. 953 AH) the historian and scholar of the science of hadīth says, "The excellences and virtues of Ali b. Hosayn b. Alī b. Abī-Tāleb Zeyn ol-Ābedīn ﷺ are more than that which can be gathered."[191]

26. Ahmad b. Hajar al-Haythamī al-Makkī (d. 974 AH) says, "Ali b. Hosayn b. Alī b. Abī-Tāleb Zeyn ol-Ābedīn ﷺ was the successor of his father in his knowledge [of the religious sciences] and in asceticism and worship... He was forgiving and overlooked [people's] faults."[192]

27. Muhammad b. Ali ash-Showkānī (d. 1255 AH), a senior magister and the chief justice and magistrate of the Yemen says, "The fame of the two imams, Zeyd b. Ali, and his father, Zeyn ol-Ābedīn ﷺ is more illustrious than fire on a flagpole."[193]

28. Shaykh Balkhī al-Qondūzī (d. 1294 AH) states, "The people of every religio-legal rite (*madhhab*) are unanimously agreed on the virtues of Ali b. Hosayn ﷺ, and no one doubts his preeminence and his imamate."[194]

29. Hāfez Muhammad Abdor-Rahmān Mobārakfūrī (d. 1353 AH), a commentator on imam Termedhī's Sahīh, says, "Ali b. Hosayn b. Alī b. Abī-Tāleb Zeyn ol-Ābedīn ﷺ was a reliable and trustworthy authority

[as a transmitter of hadīth] (*thaqa thabt*), one who was dedicated to the devotion and adoration of God ﷻ (*'ābed*), a magister (a scholar of the religious science; a theologian cum jurisdoctor; *faqīh*), and a renowned man of virtuous accomplishments."[195]

30. Shaykh Mostafā Rashdī (d. 1309 AH) says, "Abū Muhammad Zeyn ol-Ābedīn Ali-Asghar's title was as-Sajjād ﷺ (the one who prostrates [often]) because he was dedicated to the ritual devotions and to the adoration of God ﷻ. He was an imam, and his virtuosity is undeniable. He was courageous and munificent, and his "impossible wonders" and extra-ordinary feats (*karāmāt*) are more numerous than can be enumerated [here]."[196]

31. Shaykh Mahmūd al-Ālūsī (d. 1342 AH), a man of letters and exegete of the Quran has called Ali b. Hosayn ﷺ "the Chief of the [Muslim] Gnostics (*ra'īs al-'ārefīn*)."[197]

32. The contemporary biographer Khayrod-Dīn Zarkalī (d. 1410 AH) writes, "Ali b. Hosayn b. Alī b. Abī-Tāleb Zeyn ol-Ābedīn ﷺ was a legend of humility and God-fearing piety (*war'*)."[198]

33. Dr. Abdos-Salām at-Tarmānīnī says, "Ali b. Hosayn ﷺ became known as the Adornment of the Worshippers [of God ﷻ] (Zeyn ol-Ābedīn) on account of his dedication to the devotion and adoration of God ﷻ. He was a scholar of the science of hadīth (i.e. he was a compendium of memorized hadīth), and was legendary in his forbearance, God-fearing piety, and generosity."[199]

34. The Egyptian author Abdor-Rahmān ash-Sharqāwī says, "Ali b. Hosayn Zeyn ol-Ābedīn ﷺ was occupied with propagating the teachings of Islam

to the people, and prompted his children to pursue the religious sciences, positioning them as righteous imams in his wake."²⁰⁰

35. The military advisor Abdol-Halīm Jandī says, "Each generation (literally, 'day') a great personality would appear in the household of Zeyn ol-Ābedīn ﷺ. [Imam] Sajjād ﷺ presented his son [Imam] Bāqer ﷺ to society, and [Imam] Bāqer ﷺ presented his son [Imam] Sādeq ﷺ to society. They were the foremost examples of those who had withdrawn themselves from the court of the ruling authority and occupied themselves with educating the people in the correct teachings of the faith, in the proper mode of courteous conduct, and generally presenting an exemplary model of behavior."²⁰¹

36. Shaykh Jāber Jazā'erī says, "This is the testimony of az-Zahrī to [the accomplishments of] Ali b. al-Hosayn ﷺ in knowledge of the religious sciences. It is related from az-Zahrī that he said, 'I did not see anyone more preeminent than Ali b. al-Hosayn ﷺ in the House of the Banī-Hāshem, nor do I know anyone more learned in the religion than he.' This testimony of az-Zahrī's [alone] is sufficient for proving the lofty status of the accomplishments and virtuosity of Ali b. al-Hosayn ﷺ in the teachings of the religion. May Almighty God ﷻ have mercy on his soul."²⁰²

37. Professor Ahmad Abū-Kaf says, "Zeyn ol-Ābedīn was the epithet which [Imam] Ali b. Hosayn ﷺ was known by. He was the only person who did not fall victim at Karbalā to the hatred and the swords of the Omayyads... so that he would remain and be able to serve as the historical antecedent for all of the Godly *owlīā* (saints, those who have spiritual proximity to God ﷻ) from the House of Prophethood. In the carnage of Karbalā, the lineage of prophethood was severed with the martyrdom of Hosayn b. Ali , the Lord of the Martyrs who dwell in

Paradise, and [the martyrdom of] his family. But with the continuation of the life of his son Ali Zeyn ol-Ābedīn ﷺ, the Adornment of the Youth of Paradise and the most preeminent of the Qūraysh, the lineage of prophethood was sustained and continued [uninterrupted]."[203]

38. Shaykh Muhammad Kheḍr Hosayn, a professor at the al-Azhar university, says: "Ali b. Hosayn ﷺ became known as the Adornment of the Worshippers [of God ﷻ] (Zeyn ol-Ābedīn) on account of his dedication to the devotion and adoration of God ﷻ. But this is not an [example of one of those] epithets which mothers and fathers place on their children at the time of their birth. [At times,] people name their children [things like] Zeyn ol-Ābedīn ﷺ, even though their child has not yet even begun to make their ritual devotions. Or they will name their son Nāseroddīn (the support of the religion), while he [turns out in practice] to weaken the pillars of the religion [instead]! [The author intends to say that this is not a recommended practice, and it is not what happened in the case of Ali b. Hosayn ﷺ, whose well-deserved title was bestowed on him by the people and not by his parents.]"[204]

39. Shaykh Yāsīn b. Ebrāhīm as-Sanhūtī ash-Shāfe'ī says, "Our Lord and Master, [Imam] Zeyn ol-Ābedīn ﷺ, may God ﷻ be pleased with him, was the manifestation of the luminosity (literally, 'the sun') of the Seal of Prophethood, and the embodiment [of the unveiling] of the Mysteries of Being, and the crystal-clear fountainhead (Kowthar) of the munificence of the Banī-Hāshem (the House of the Prophet)... He had an exalted [spiritual] rank. He was magnanimous, munificent, and was the object of [the people's] reverence. He was a great scholar and was an upright and trustworthy authority [as a transmitter of hadīth] (*thaqa^{t} thabt^{an} qūyūm^{an}*)."[205]

5. Imam Muhammad b. Ali al-Bāqer

A large number of Sunni scholars have stipulated the appellation of *al-bāqer* (The Splitter [of the Kernel of Religious Knowledge]) [to Imam Muhammad b. Ali ﷺ] and have stated that the reason for this designation is because he [was able to] split knowledge [relating to the religious or sacred sciences] and to gain access to its hidden inner meaning.[206]

The following is a selection of some of what the Associates of the Prophet ﷺ, the generation of the Followers, and Sunni scholarship has said about Imam al-Bāqer ﷺ.

1. Muhammad b. Monkader (d. 130 AH), one of the scholars of hadīth science in Medina from the generation of the Followers says, "I had not seen anyone more preeminent in virtue than Ali b. al-Hosayn until I came across his son Muhammad al-Bāqer] ﷺ."[207]

2. Muhammad b. 'Atā', a scholar of the science of hadīth, says, "I have never seen anyone the like of Abī-Ja'far [Muhammad b. Ali] ﷺ in comparison to whom [the stature of other] scholars of religion (*olamā*) diminished. Hakam [b. 'Otayba, the renowned Kūfan magister] was as a student compared to him."[208]

3. Eben Sa'd (d. 203 AH), the great historian, has said, "He was [a] reliable and trustworthy [transmitter of hadīth] (*thiqa*), and had a great knowledge of hadīth and of the religious sciences."[209]

4. Muhammad b. Talha ash-Shāfe'ī (d. 652 AH) says, "Imam Muhammad al-Bāqer ﷺ was the splitter of knowledge [relating to the religious or sacred sciences], the compiler of knowledge, and the explainer and exalter of [the intricacies of] the knowledge of the religious sciences… His heart

was pure; his conduct was exemplary; his soul was untainted; and his mode of courteous conduct was noble. He dedicated his time to devotion to God ❋ and steadied his step by means of God-fearing piety (*taqwā*), and the signs of his proximity to God ❋ and of the purity of his choice of [a] God[ly life] were evident on his person. Virtues rush toward him and desirable attributes turn to him."[210]

5. Eben Abī'l-Hadīd (d. 656 AH), the great Sunni scholar of the Shāfe'ī rite and the author of a great multi-volume commentary on the *Nahj ol-Balāgha*, writes, "Muhammad b. Ali ❋ ... was the Lord and Master of the magisters (*foqahā*) of the Hejāz. The people learned the religious sciences from him and from his son [Imam] Ja'far [as-Sādeq]. His epithet was "al-Bāqer", and he was [indeed] a splitter of knowledge. It was the Prophet ❋ who gave him this designation [by way of a prophecy], and no one had this title before this."[211]

6. Mohīoddīn an-Nawawī, the great Shāfe'ite magister, says, "Muhammad al-Bāqer ❋ was so named because he split [apart] knowledge [of the sacred sciences], entered into it and attained to an exalted and gratified station therein."[212]

7. The biographer Eben Khalkān (d. 681 AH) writes, "Muhammad al-Bāqer ❋ was a Lord and a great scholar; he was called "al-Baqer" because he attained to a vast amount of knowledge."[213]

8. The greatest of the Sunni biographers, a prosopographer and a historian, Shamsoddīn adh-Dhahabī (d. 748 AH) says,
    8.1. "Abū-Ja'far al-Bāqer ❋ was a Lord and an imam (leader). He was a person who combined theory and practice, distinction and nobility, dignity and authority, and he was worthy of the office of the caliphate... He was known as al-Bāqer, because he [was able to]

split knowledge [relating to the religious or sacred sciences] and to gain access to its hidden inner meaning. He was an imam, a mojtahed (one who strives to derive correct beliefs, laws and codes of moral conduct from their scriptural sources), a reciter of the Book of God ﷻ, and was greatly respected."[214]

8.2. Dhahabī also states, "Abū-Ja'far al-Bāqer Muhammad b. Ali. B. al-Hosayn b. Alī b. Abī-Tāleb ﷺ was a Hāshemite, an Ālid, a Medinan imam; he was a reliable and trustworthy authority [as a transmitter of hadīth] (*thaqa thabt*) and one of the elders [of the community]. He was the Lord of the Banī-Hāshem of his generation who was known as al-Bāqer, meaning he [was able to] split knowledge [relating to the religious or sacred sciences] and to gain access to its inner hidden meaning. It is related that he used to establish a thousand cycles (*rak'a*) of the ritual devotions in [a single] day and night [cycle]. Nasāī and others consider him to be one of the scholars of the religious sciences of the generation of the Followers (*tābe'īn*)."[215]

9. The great biographer and Quranic exegete Eben Kathīr (d. 774 AH) states: "Abū-Ja'far al-Bāqer Muhammad b. Ali. B. al-Hosayn b. Alī b. Abī-Tāleb ﷺ ... was known as al-Bāqer, meaning he [was able to] split knowledge [relating to the religious or sacred sciences] and derive sacred laws therefrom. He was an invoker (*dhāker*) [of the remembrance of God ﷻ], was humble, had patience and forbearance, and was of the stock of prophethood. He had an exalted lineage, [social rank and spiritual] station. He understood [the futility of (?) engaging in] dangerous causes, shed tears easily and avoided hostility and discord."[216]

10. Shamsoddīn Muhammad b. Tūtūn (Eben Batūta) al-Hanafī (d. 953 AH) the historian and scholar of the science of hadīth says, "Muhammad

b. Ali al-Bāqer ﷺ was a descendent of the Prophet ﷺ, a scholar and a great man."²¹⁷

11. Ahmad b. Hajar al-Haythamī al-Makkī (d. 974 AH) says, "Abū-Ja'far Muhammad b. Ali al-Bāqer ﷺ was the heir of the Imams in ritual devotions and worship, in his understanding and knowledge of the religion, and in his asceticism and self-abnegation. They called him al-Bāqer because it is said that *baqar al-arḍ* means 'he split open the earth, and exposed what was hidden therein.' He split open the hidden treasures of the teachings of Islam, the true laws of Islam, and the wisdom and subtle aspects of the [religious] sciences and made them manifest, such that they were no longer hidden to anyone other than those who have no vision or are inwardly corrupted. This is why he was considered to be someone who was the splitter of knowledge [relating to the religious or sacred sciences], the compiler of knowledge, and the explainer and exalter of [the intricacies of] the knowledge of the religious sciences… His heart was pure; his conduct was exemplary; his soul was untainted; and his mode of courteous conduct was noble. He dedicated his time to devotion to God ﷻ. He has a book about the stages of the gnostics that has reached us whose beauty is beyond words (literally, beyond the ability of the tongue)."²¹⁸

12. The great linguist Zobeydī (d. 1205 AH) says, "Abū-Ja'far al-Bāqer Muhammad ﷺ b. Ali. B. al-Hosayn b. Alī b. Abī-Tāleb was known as al-Bāqer, meaning he delved deeply and [was able to] split knowledge [relating to the religious or sacred sciences] and had the power of oratory. He understood the knowledge of the religious sciences, differentiated its principles and derived its secondary derivations."²¹⁹

13. Shaykh Mostafā Rashdī (d. 1309 AH) says, "Imam Muhammad al-Bāqer ﷺ was a renowned and exalted dignitary. No one of his generation

matched him in his knowledge of the religion, knowledge of the *sonna* (the exemplary model of the Prophet ﷺ), or knowledge of God ﷻ. The imams of the generation of the Followers (*tābe'īn*) have transmitted hadīth reports which were narrated by him."[220]

14. Muhammad Abdor-Ra'ūf al-Manāwī (d. 1331 AH), a commentator on hadīth, considers Imām Bāqer ؏ to be one of the magisters (*foqahā*) of the beginning of the first century and a *mojadded* [the inspired renewer of religious thought and practice which make their appearance at the beginning of each century according to a hadīth report of the Prophet's ﷺ]. He considers Imām Reḍā ؏ to be the fulfillment of this prophecy at the beginning of the second Islamic century.[221]

15. Shaykh Yūsof b. Esmāīl an-Nabhānī al-Beyrūtī (d. 1350 AH) who was the chief magistrate of Beirut says, "[Imam] Muhammad al-Bāqer ؏, may God ﷻ be pleased with him, was one of our imams (leaders) and masters [descended] from the noble House of the Prophet ﷺ, and a unique and great scholar of religion."[222]

16. Ali b. Muhammad al-Fekrī al-Hosaynī al-Qaherī (d. 1372 AH) says, "It has been said that of the progeny of [the Imams] al-Hasan ؏ and al-Hosayn ؏ none has surpassed [Imam] Abī-Ja'far Muhammad b. Ali al-Bāqer ؏ in their understanding of the religion, knowledge of the *sonna* (the exemplary model of the Prophet ﷺ), the Quranic sciences, biography (*sīra*), and the Islamic mode of courteous conduct (*adab*). He transmitted the knowledge of the religion from the remnants of [the generation of] the Associates of the Prophet ﷺ and the notables of the generation of the Followers, and the substance of his speech concerning the sacred sciences became the subject of the transmitted sciences, and elegies have been composed in his honor."[223]

17. Shaykh Yāsīn b. Ebrāhīm as-Sanhūtī ash-Shāfe'ī says, "Our Lord and Master, [Imam] Muhammad b. Ali al-Bāqer ﷺ, may God ﷻ be pleased with him, was a leader of the generation of the Followers and was a magisterial notable, upon whose leadership and splendor there is unanimity."²²⁴

18. Shaykh Muhammad Khedr Hosayn, a professor at the al-Azhar university, says: "[Imam] Muhammad b. Ali al-Bāqer ﷺ was one of the great scholars of the religious sciences... In addition to his place in the Quranic sciences, [Imam] Muhammad b. Ali al-Bāqer ﷺ had an exalted status in the high virtues of the Islamic mode of courteous conduct (*adab*), in the scholarly striving for the derivation of law (*ejtehād*), and in his conforming to the way of God ﷻ."²²⁵

6. Imam Ja'far b. Muhammad as-Sādeq

The various facets to Imam Ja'far as-Sādeq's ﷺ personality, and especially the various aspects of his vast scholarship, were manifested more than were those of the rest of the Imams; and this is because of the special conditions of his time which were conducive to the religious and intellectual development of society. For this reason, Imam Ja'far as-Sādeq's ﷺ religious and intellectual positions were the subject of much attention, both of the Sunni community, but also of the orientalists of the West. With this in mind, a group of orientalists in a research center in Strasburg proceeded to carry out some research into the personality of Imam Ja'far as-Sādeq ﷺ and published the results of their findings in a book entitled *The Great Muslim Scientist and Philosopher - Imam Ja'far Ibn Muhammad As-Sadiq*. According to the findings of this book, Imam Ja'far as-Sādeq ﷺ is the source of many of the theories in the empirical sciences which were to be proven by Western scientists many centuries later.

Some books have also been written by Sunni scholars regarding Imam Ja'far as-Sādeq ﷺ, such as the ones by Muhammad Abu-Zahra and Abdol-Halīm al-Jandī.

The following is a selection of some of what the Associates of the Prophet ﷺ, the generation of the Followers, and Sunni scholarship has said about Imam Ja'far as-Sādeq ﷺ.

1. Mālek b. Anas (d. 179 AH), the eponymous founder of the Mālekī religio-legal rite (*madhhab*) states, "I knew Ja'far as-Sādeq ﷺ and saw him occupied in one of three states: in the state of performing his ritual devotions, in fasting mode, or while he was occupied with the recitation of the Quran. He never recited hadīth reports from the Prophet ﷺ unless he was in a state of ritual purity. He was among the scholars of religion who lived an ascetic life and a life dedicated to the ritual devotions and to the adoration of God ﷻ, and who have a pious fear of God ﷻ. I made the Major Pilgrimage (*hajj*) with him once; he entered into a state of ritual consecration (*ihrām*) in the Masjed ash-Shajara, and when he was in the stage of pronouncing the *labbayk* ("I am at thy command, [my Lord]."), he would pass out. I told him, "There are no two ways about it, you must pronounce the words *labbayk*! Because he respected me and talked openly with me, he told me, "I am afraid to say *labbayk* and for there to come a reply in return *lā labbayk*! [negating my pledge]." His grandfather Ali b. al-Hosayn Zeyn ol-Ābedīn ﷺ would also faint when he was in the stage of pronouncing *allāhomma labbayk*, and would fall to the ground from the back of a camel and injure his face. May God ﷻ be please with them all."[226]

2. The following is related from Abū-Hanīfa, the eponymous founder of the Hanafī religio-legal rite (*madhhab*), who was a student of Imam Ja'far as-Sādeq's[227] ﷺ: Abū-Hanīfa was asked 'Who is the most learned person

in the religious sciences?' He replied, 'I have not seen anyone more learned in the religious sciences than Ja'far as-Sādeq ﷺ. When the Abbāsid caliph al-Mansūr sent Ja'far as-Sādeq ﷺ to the town of Hīra, he summoned me and told me, 'The people are taken by Ja'far as-Sādeq ﷺ; therefore, prepare some difficult questions to test him with. And so I prepared forty difficult questions. al-Mansūr then summoned me again and when I entered into his court, Ja'far as-Sādeq ﷺ was seated to his right. When I looked at the two of them, the awe which he inspired in me was more than that which the caliph inspired. al-Mansūr addressed Ja'far as-Sādeq ﷺ, saying, 'O Abā Abdollāh, do you know this man?' Ja'far as-Sādeq ﷺ said, 'Yes, he is Abū-Hanīfa.' Al-Mansūr then told me to ask my questions of Abā Abdollāh (Imam Ja'far as-Sādeq ﷺ) . I proceeded to ask my questions one by one. And Ja'far as-Sādeq would in turn answer me by saying that you (people of the Irāq) rule on this point in this way, and the people of Medina also have the same ruling, and we the People of the House [of the Prophet ﷺ] (*ahl al-bayt* ﷺ) also rule in the same way. He would agree with our rulings on some occasions, would agree with the rulings of the Medinans on others, and on some occasions would reject both our rulings. And this situation continued until I had asked all forty of my questions and he had answered them all in this fashion.' Abū-Hanīfa then says, 'Is it not the case that the most knowledgeable of men is [one who is] aware of the differences of opinion [that exist] between the different people [of different regions]?'"[228]

3. Mohīoddīn an-Nawawī (d. 676 AH) has referred to Imam Ja'far as-Sādeq ﷺ as the Imam of the Household (*imām al-'etra*).

4. The historian and prosopographer Abū-Hātam Muhammad b. Hebbān (d. 354 AH) writes, "Ja'far ﷺ b. Muhammad b. Ali b. al-Hosayn b. Alī b. Abī-Tāleb, may God ﷻ grant them all Heaven, had the agnomen (*konya*) Abā Abdollāh. He was one of the great men of the People of the

House [of the Prophet ﷺ] (*ahl al-bayt* ؑ) who was accomplished in the sacred and profane sciences and in the art of the Islamic mode of courteous conduct (*adab*)."²²⁹

5. Hākem-e Neyshāpūrī (d. 405 AH), the great scholar of the science of hadīth, says, "The most sound and most authoritative provenance titles (*asānīd*) of hadīth reports of the People of the House [of the Prophet ﷺ] (*ahl al-bayt* ؑ) are [those contained in] the hadīth reports of Ja'far ؑ b. Muhammad b. Ali b. al-Hosayn b. Ali b. Abī-Tāleb, [which have reached us] by way of his father Muhammad b. Ali ؑ back from his ancestor Ali b. Abī-Tāleb ؑ."²³⁰

6. Eben Abdol-Birr (d. 463 AH), a Sunnite scholar of the science of hadīth, says, "Ja'far b. Muhammad ؑ, known as as-Sādeq, was a reliable and trustworthy authority [as a transmitter of hadīth] (*thaqa thabt*), had a sound intellect and was wise, was humble, and was a renowned man of virtuous accomplishments. Most of his words were words of wisdom. He was the most intelligent person and neglected [the priorities and values of] the hereafter less than everyone else."²³¹

7. Abol-Faraj Abdor-Rahmān b. Ali b. Muhammad b. Jowzī (d. 597 AH) has said, "Ja'far b. Muhammad ؑ was a scholar of the religious sciences, an ascetic, and one who was dedicated to the devotion and adoration of God ﷻ (*ābed*)."²³²

8. Muhammad b. Talha ash-Shāfe'ī (d. 652 AH) says, "Imam Ja'far as-Sādeq ؑ was one of the luminaries of the House of the Prophet ﷺ, had a vast amount of knowledge, was dedicated to the devotion and continual invocation of God ﷻ, was an ascetic and a frequent reciter of the Quran, which brought about a [deep] understanding of its meaning, the extraction of a great many treasures from the depth of its oceans, and

attaining to [an understanding of] its many wonders. He spent his time in obeisance to God ﷻ to the point that he assayed [the current state of] his soul [relative] to the [unalloyed practice of] obeisance to God ﷻ. Being in his company reminded one of the world of the hereafter, and listening to his words made one reconsider one's worldly [orientations and] desires. Following his teachings ensured one's attainment of Heaven. The luminosity of his countenance was telling of the fact that he was of the lineage of prophethood, and the purity of his behavior spoke of his being of the tribe of the prophets."[233]

9. Eben Abī'l-Hadīd (d. 656 AH), the exegete of the *Nahj ol-Balāgha* writes, "Ja'far b. Muhammad ﷺ is someone whose knowledge of the religious sciences has filled the whole world [with light]. It is reported that Abū-Haīfa and Sofyān ath-Thūrī were among his students. The presence of these two among his students is sufficient for proving this claim: it is for this reason that these two are said to have adhered to the religio-legal rite (*madhhab*) of the Zaydīs."[234]

10. Mohīyoddīn an-Nawāwī (d. 681 AH), the great Shāfe'ī magister (*faqīh*), after issuing his *fatwā* (authoritative legal opinion) recommending the visitations of graves in the Baqī' cemetery[235] during any day of the week, mentions the names of eight people as those who have ritually pure graves and the visitations of whose graves are recommended. Among these eight names are the names of four of the Imams of the Shī'a: Hasan b. Ali ﷺ, Ali b. Hosayn ﷺ, Muhammad b. Ali ﷺ, and Ja'far b. Muhammad ﷺ."[236]

11. Eben Khalkān writes the following about Imam Ja'far as-Sādeq ﷺ: "Imam Ja'far as-Sādeq ﷺ was one of the luminaries of the House of the Prophet ﷺ. He was called *as-sādeq* (the truthful) on account of his truthfulness. His virtues are so famous that there is no need to mention

them... He was buried in a grave in which his father before him Muhammad al-Bāqer was buried, and his grandfather Zeyn ol-Ābedīn ﷺ was buried, and his grandfather's uncle, Hasan b. Ali was buried. What a noble and bounteous grave!"[237]

12. The great biographer, prosopographer and historian Shamsoddīn adh-Dhahabī (d. 748 AH) says, "Imam Ja'far as-Sādeq ﷺ was one of the great men who was descended from the noble House of the Prophet ﷺ... His virtues are numerous; who can be better than him in the science of hadīth?"[238]

13. The biographer Salāhoddīn as-Saftī (d. 764 AH) says, "He was a great leader and was known as "The Truthful" (as-Sādeq ﷺ) ... He had an abundance of virtuous accomplishments and was worthy of the office of the caliphate on account [of them and because] of his noble lineage, which was of the noble House of the Prophet ﷺ. His excellences were copious. God ﷻ made him the subject of His mercy... He was buried in the Baqī' cemetery (in Medīna) in a grave in which his father before him Muhammad al-Bāqer ﷺ was buried, and his grandfather Zeyn ol-Ābedīn ﷺ was buried, and his grandfather's uncle, Hasan b. Ali ﷺ was buried, may God ﷻ be pleased with them all. May God ﷻ grant him of His bounties; what a noble and bounteous grave! He was called as-Sādeq (the truthful) on account of his truthfulness."[239]

14. The biographer Eben Hajar al-Asqalānī (d. 852 AH) writes, "Ja'far b. Muhammad ﷺ was known as as-Sādeq on account of his sincerity; he spoke the truth, was a scholar of the religious sciences, and an imam."[240]

15. Allāme Eben Sabbāgh al-Makkī (d. 855 AH), the leader of the Mālekī religio-legal rite (*madhhab*) of his era, writes about Imam Ja'far as-Sādeq ﷺ as follows:

3 The Evidence

15.1. "Ja'far as-Sādeq ﷺ became the *wasī* (heir, executor and inheritor), successor (*khalīfa*) and the upholder of the Imāmate from among the children of [his father] Muhammad b. Ali al-Bāqer ﷺ. He was more preeminent than his brothers in the excellence of his virtues, was of better repute, and had attained to a higher [spiritual] station. [The light of] his knowledge has spread to everywhere mankind has treaded, and his name is known in every town. Our religious scholars have related more hadīth reports on his authority than from anyone else in the House of the Prophet ﷺ."[241]

15.2. Eben Sabbāgh has also stated, "The virtues of Abī [*sic*] Ja'far as-Sādeq ﷺ are better, and his attributes of nobility are perfected, and his nobility has had currency on the forehead of the times, and glory and dignity have become manifest in his works and achievements."[242]

16. Muhammad Khāje-ye Pārsā-ye Bokhārī (d. 865 AH), the magister (*faqīh*), scholar of the science of hadīth, and Sūfī says, "There is consensus concerning the nobility of lineage and greatness of [Imam] as-Sādeq. Shaykh Abū Abdor-Rahmān as-Salamī states in his book Tabaqāt al-Mashāyekh as-Sūfīya (Stations of the Sūfī Elders): "Ja'far as-Sādeq ﷺ had preeminence over his contemporaries from the House of the Prophet ﷺ. He had a deep knowledge of the religion and lived a completely ascetic [lifestyle]. He was devout and abstained completely from the desires and dictates of the lower self. He was an exemplary model in the high virtues of the Islamic mode of courteous conduct (*adab*)... his virtues are countless.

17. Shamsoddīn Muhammad b. Tūtūn (Eben Batūta) al-Hanafī (d. 953 AH) the historian and scholar of the science of hadīth says, "[Imam] as-Sādeq ﷺ was a nobleman from the noble lineage of the House of the Prophet ﷺ, and was known as as-Sādeq because of the sincerity and

reliability of his words. The excellences of his virtues are too well-known to require a retelling [here]."²⁴³

18. Ahmad b. Hajar al-Haythamī al-Makkī (d. 974 AH) says, "[Imam] as-Sādeq ﷺ became the wasī (heir, executor and inheritor) and successor (*khalīfa*) of Muhammad b. Ali al-Bāqer ﷺ. [The light of] his knowledge has spread to everywhere mankind has treaded, and his name is known in every land. The greatest names in religious scholarship were his students."²⁴⁴

19. Shaykh Yūsof b. Esmāīl an-Nabhānī al-Beyrūtī (d. 1350 AH) who was the chief magistrate of Beirut says, "[Imam] Ja'far as-Sādeq ﷺ was a nobleman from among our Lords and Masters, i.e. from the noble lineage of the House of the Prophet ﷺ, the *ahl al-bayt* ﷺ."²⁴⁵

20. The famous Quranic exegete Shaykh Mahmūd al-Ālūsī (d. 1271 AH) writes:

    20.1. "[Imam] Ja'far as-Sādeq ﷺ was devout, righteous, and a reliable and trustworthy [transmitter of hadith] (*thiqa*)."²⁴⁶

    20.2. After presenting certain concepts in a commentary on some *āyas* of the Quran, Shaykh Ālūsī states, "these are the thoughts of [Imam] Ja'far as-Sādeq ﷺ, taken from the ocean of the *ahl al-bayt* ﷺ (the People of the House [of the Prophet ﷺ]), and the Master of the House is more aware of that which is in the House."²⁴⁷

21. Hāfez Muhammad Abdor-Rahmān Mobārakfūrī (d. 1353 AH), a commentator on imam Termedhī's *Sahīh*, says, "[Imam] Ja'far as-Sādeq ﷺ was a reliable and trust-worthy [transmitter of hadith] (*thiqa*), was truthful, was a master of the Quranic sciences (*faqīh*), and was an imam."²⁴⁸

22. We find the following written in the book *at-Towfīq ar-Rabbānī fī ar-radd 'alā ibn Taymīya al-Harrānī* (Divine Success in the Repudiation of Eben Taymīya al-Harrānī) which is authored by a group of contemporary Sunni scholars: "The first proof is derived from the words of [Imam] Ja'far as-Sādeq ﷺ, may God ﷻ be pleased with him, who is endowed with flawless virtues, hails from the noblest lineage, is a master of the scholars of the religious sciences, and the inheritor of the best of the prophets."[249]

23. The contemporary biographer Zarkalī and Dr. Abdor-Rahmān 'Amīra (whose madhhab or religio-legal rite and aqīda or creedal basis is Ebādī) and who is the chair of the Department of Islamic Studies in the Sultan Qaboos University in Muscat), describes [Imam] Ja'far as-Sādeq ﷺ: "He was the best of the generation of the Followers (*tābe'īn*) and had an exalted position as a master of the Quranic sciences. A number of scholars, including Abū-Hanīfa and Imam Mālek b. Anas learned from him. His epithet was as-Sādeq because he was never heard to utter a lie. He was courageous in the face of the Abbāsid caliphs and stood up for justice."[250]

24. Seyyed Abbās al-Makkī, a contemporary author, says: "[Imam] Ja'far as-Sādeq ﷺ was one of the twelve Imams [of the Shī'a] and was a dignitary of the House of the Prophet ﷺ. His epithet was as-Sādeq because of his truthfulness. His fame is more illustrious than fire on a flagpole. And why should this not be the case when he is the progeny of the Master of every community? ... Scholars thronged outside the door of his house. He was the beneficiary of the luminous light of the elect. He spoke [in terms] of the difficulties [of attaining to] the mysteries [or high teachings of the religion] and of real science."[251]

25. Seyyed Muhammad b. Abdol-Ghaffār al-Hāshemī al-Afghānī says, "[Imam] Ja'far as-Sādeq ﷺ was a deep ocean of knowledge and had four thousand students[252] who have transmitted hadīth reports on his authority, including the great Imam, Abū-Hanīfa and Imam Mālek b. Anas and Imam Sofyan ath-Thūrī, as well as many other great scholars. [Imam] Ja'far as-Sādeq ﷺ lived an ascetic lifestyle of piety and self-restraint. He had answered the call of God ﷻ and was a God-fearing man. He was clearly one who was gifted with "impossible wonders" and extra-ordinary feats (*karāmāt*), concerning which much has been written in our books.'[253]

26. Shaykh Muhammad Abū-Zahra al-Mālekī (d. 1394 AH), a professor at the al-Azhar seminary and the greatest scholar of the religious sciences of his era, has written about [Imam] Ja'far as-Sādeq ﷺ on numerous occasions in his works. He also has a book dedicated to the Imam called *Al-Imām as-Sādeq*. Prior to writing this book, Shaykh Abū-Zahra had already penned seven books about seven great scholars of Islam, namely, Abū-Hanīfa, Mālek b. Anas, Ahmad b. Hanbal, Muhammad b. Edrīs ash-Shāfe'ī, Zeyd b. Alī b. Hosayn, Eben Taymīya and Eben Hazm. In the introduction to his book *Al-Imām as-Sādeq* he states,

26.1."We determined to write a book, with God ﷻ aid and succor, about Imam Ja'far as-Sādeq ﷺ. Before this, we had already written seven books about seven other great imams. The writing of the book on Imam Ja'far as-Sādeq ﷺ was not postponed on account of his being lower in rank or importance than the other seven. To the contrary: he is prior to most of them chronologically, and has a special preeminence over the greats among them. Imam Abū-Hanīfa has related hadīth reports on his authority and describes him as the most knowledgeable scholar of comparative sacred jurisprudence, considering his understanding (*fiqh*) to be more expansive than the other magisters (*foqahā*). Imam Mālek b. Anas also went to him to learn from him and to take down hadīth reports. Let it be said that someone who is in the position of professor to students such as Imam Abū-Hanīfa and Imam Mālek – such a distinction is sufficient unto him as an outstanding virtue. [The writing of the intellectual biography of] such a person cannot [be said to] be postponed on account of a shortcoming [on his part]; and no other has [a claim of] superiority over his, such that they would be considered to be prior to him [in rank]. Rather, Imam Ja'far as-Sādeq ﷺ is even higher than the ranks of these considerations. He was the grandson of Ali b. al-Hosayn Zeyn ol-Ābedīn ﷺ, who was the master of the people of Medina in his era in terms of the excellence of his virtues, nobility, religiosity, and knowledge. Eben Shahāb az-Zahrī and many other notables of the generation of the Followers (*tābe'īn*) were students of his. Imam Ja'far as-Sādeq ﷺ is the son of Imam Muhammad al-Bāqer ﷺ, who split [the nut of] science and accessed the substance of its kernel. Imam Ja'far as-Sādeq ﷺ is one who combines in his person innate nobility with the dignity that comes with the nobility of lineage and of one who hails from the Hashemite House of Muhammad ﷺ."[254]

26.2. In another one of his works Shaykh Abū-Zahra states, "Imam Ja'far as-Sādeq ﷺ was munificent and tolerant and would not reciprocate a wrong done against him with another wrong; rather, he would respond with a good turn... He was a grateful servant of God... He was forbearing, humble, pious and devout... It is perhaps impossible to find someone who combined gratitude and patience and forbearance in his person like Imam Ja'far as-Sādeq ﷺ. The righteous sons of Alī b. Abī-Tāleb ﷺ were all courageous and did not flinch from death; and this was especially the case with Imam Ja'far as-Sādeq whose heart was filled with [the verities of] faith and had no room for the urgings of the lower self; he feared only God ﷻ, and was not afraid of anyone else, no matter how powerful he might be. He was also courageous against those who claimed to be his followers but who had distorted the teachings of Islam. He displayed courage in the face of the insubordination [to God ﷻ] and the displays of the power of the Abbāsid caliph Mansūr: when Mansūr asked him why God ﷻ had created flies, he responded: "In order to humiliate tyrants and oppressors." Imam Ja'far as-Sādeq ﷺ had wit and cunning in abundance, and it was perhaps thanks to his cunning that he was able to avoid getting entangled in the [political] currents of the day and the leadership of the various political movements of his day."[255]

26.3. In yet another one of his works Shaykh Abū-Zahra states, "Imam Ja'far as-Sādeq ﷺ was a stout branch of the great tree of the House of Hāshem who found the opportunity [in the respite of the suppression of his House provided by the infighting during the interregnum of the Omayyad/ Abbāsid transition] to turn to science and strive in it despite the nobility of his lineage which went back to the Prophet ﷺ himself. He fused [the wisdoms of] the schools of Medina and Iraq. His background was conducive to the scholarly life as his father was Imām Muhammad al-Bāqer ﷺ, who in turn was the son of Imam Ali b. al-Hosayn Zeyn ol-Ābedīn ﷺ, a leader among the scholars of Medina. He was a source of reference and one whose legal opinions were authoritative. He combined in his person the nobility of lineage and the nobility of character and honor and respect of the House of Hāshem... It is said [of Imam Ja'far as-Sādeq's ﷺ father that he became known as al-Bāqer ﷺ (The Splitter) because when he became known as a dignitary of science and scholarship, they said of his accomplishments that it was as if he split science in two and was able to reach the inward meaning of its ultimate mysteries... Imam Ja'far as-Sādeq ﷺ grew up and received his training in a household such as this."[256]

26.4. And finally: "Despite the fact that Mālek [b. Anas, the eponymous founder of the Mālekī *madhhab*] did not approve of and in fact was against the way of the Ālids, he was nonetheless the student of Imam Ja'far as-Sādeq ﷺ, and this [his personal position] did not stand in the way of his acquiring knowledge and learning from the Imam, and to remember him in the best possible way that a student can remember his master."[257]

27. Shaykh Yāsīn b. Ebrāhīm as-Sanhūtī ash-Shāfe'ī says, "It suffices us to say that Imam Ja'far as-Sādeq ﷺ, may God ﷻ be pleased with him, was an imam who was the heir to the Station of Prophethood and Truthfulness. Rays of knowledge and the true teachings [of Islam] radiated from his countenance because his great grandfather was the Lord of the Martyrs Imam Hosayn ﷺ ... He was graced with many "impossible wonders" and extra-ordinary feats (*karāmāt*), and with legendary unveilings (*mokāshefāt*) [of the Invisible World or of the world that is beyond the ken of ordinary human perception (*al-ghayb*)]."[258]

28. Shaykh Abdol-Wahhāb Abdol-Latīf, a professor at the al-Azhar seminary, says, "[Imam] Ja'far as-Sādeq ﷺ, may God ﷻ be pleased with him and his ancestors, was a notable from the generation of the Followers (*tābe'īn*). He was full of God-fearing piety (*war'*), and was well-spoken, and lived a simple life dedicated to the devotion and adoration of God ﷻ ('*ābed*).

29. Seyyed Muhammad b. Abī-Bakr b. Abdollāh al-Alawī al-Hadramī describes Imam Ja'far as-Sādeq ﷺ as follows: "He had valuable things to say concerning the understanding of the Islamic conception of monotheism (*towhīd*), [the inner] truths [accessible through devotion], general Islamic teachings (*ma'āref*), and other branches of the Quranic sciences. [The light of] his knowledge has spread to everywhere mankind

has treaded, and his name is known in every land. He would say, 'Ask me while I am still in your midst, for after I am gone, none will relate hadīth reports for you as I have done.'"²⁵⁹

30. Abū'l-Fowz Muhammad b. Amin says, "[Imam] Ja'far as-Sādeq ﷺ was the heir and legatee (*wasi*) of his father from among his brothers. Reports on such a [wide] variety of sciences as having been reported from [Imam] Ja'far as-Sādeq ﷺ have not been related from anyone else. He was an *imam* (leader) in the science of hadīth."²⁶⁰

31. Dr. Abdos-Salām at-Tarmānīnī says, "[Imam] Ja'far as-Sādeq ﷺ was known as as-Sādeq because of his truthfulness... He was one of the greats of the generation of the Followers (*tābe'īn*) and had a high rank in the religious sciences. Mālek [b. Anas] and Abū-Hanīfa and Wāsel b. 'Ata' and many other scholars were his students. The religio-legal corpus and its magisterium (reading feqhicity for *feqh*) of the Shī'a [rite] revolves around him and his father Muhammad b. Ali... He lived his life righteously and dedicated his life to science. He was an exemplary magister (*faqīh*). The Emāmī (Twelver) Shī'a consider him to be the founder of their religio-legal rite (*madhhab*), which is why it is known as the Ja'farī *madhhab*."²⁶¹

32. Bāqer Amīn al-Ward, a defense attorney and a member of the 'Union of Arab Historians' describes "[Imam] Ja'far as-Sādeq ﷺ as follows: "He was one of the greats of the generation of the Followers (*tābe'īn*) and had a high rank in the religious sciences. He was a scientist, a sage, an ascetic, and well-versed in [all of] the religious sciences. One of the scientific principles of the imam is the doctrine that permissibility (*ebāha'*) is the default state of things which changes if and only if a restriction (*nahy*) has been ordained against it. Mālek [b. Anas] and Abū-Hanīfa and many others were his students. His epithet was as-Sādeq because he was never

heard to utter a lie. Reports of his dealings with the Abbāsid caliphs reveals that he stood up against them courageously for the cause of justice."²⁶²

33. Shaykh Ahmad Mohiyyoddīn 'Ajūz says, "The followers of the Imāmīya *madhhab* are those who believe in the imāmate of twelve people from the House of the Prophet ﷺ. The Imāmīya are the largest sect of the Shī'a whose members are distributed [primarily] in Iran, Iraq and Lebanon. Their imam in religious jurisprudence (*fiqh*) and in the ordinance of the faith (*ahkām*) is [Imam] Ja'far as-Sādeq, who is the sixth of the Imams of the blessed Imams of the *ahl al-bayt* ﷺ. He is one of the greatest adepts. He lived a simple ascetic life. His religious knowledge was vast, and he had an exalted status in the high virtues of the Islamic mode of courteous conduct (*adab*). He was devout and God-fearing and abstained completely from the desires and dictates of the lower self. In addition to being one of the greatest mojtaheds (one who strives to derive correct beliefs, laws and codes of moral conduct from their scriptural sources) and a source of reference and emulation in the ordinance of the faith (*ahkām*), [Imam] Ja'far as-Sādeq ﷺ was an adept in the sciences of the Invisible World (or of the world that is beyond the ken of ordinary human perception) such as divination and alchemy, in which he was a master. His knowledge and learning were extensive, deep, exact and superior. Jāber b. al-Hayyān learned alchemy at his door."²⁶³

34. The famous contemporary author Abdor-Rahmān ash-Sharqāwī says, "The people of that era were not unanimous in their love of a personality such as Ja'far b. Muhammad ﷺ. He was known to them as Ja'far as-Sādeq as his soul was pure, the horizons of his vision were expansive, and he had a big and compassionate heart. If he showed anger, he would seek the forgiveness of others. His insight was sharp, a smile was [frequently seen] on his face, tears came easily to him, his words were agreeable, he

was good-natured, he was trustworthy, God-fearing, and overtook all in righteousness and virtue. He was of the noble House of the Prophet ﷺ."²⁶⁴

35. The military advisor Abdol-Halīm Jandī says, "Ja'far ؏ the son of Muhammad al-Bāqer ؏, the son of [Ali b. al-Hosayn] Zeyn ol-Ābedīn ؏ was a tall tree whose every leaf contained the exalted attributes of the *ahl al-bayt* ؏ (the People of the House [of the Prophet ﷺ]) which had grown anew in three successive generation: himself, his father and his grand-father. When he attained to the office of the imāmate and began his teachings, he was held in high esteem by those in power."²⁶⁵

36. Brigadier General Abdor-Razzāq Mohammd al-Aswad says, "Ja'far as-Sādeq ؏ sought knowledge with all his being, making every possible effort in its cause. He acquired the knowledge of the Quran and the knowledge of the abrogating and abrogated [verses], and acquired hadīth reports from their source. He was well-acquainted with every aspect of the theory and derivation [of sacred law] in every chapter of the sacred canon (*fiqh*)... to the point where he became the master of the religious sciences in his own era. He was of the greatest imams of his era in the Quranic sciences; he was a source of reference and emulation to whom people would travel from afar for the sake of acquiring knowledge... Ja'far as-Sādeq ؏ sought knowledge and settled for nothing less."²⁶⁶

37. Dr. Muhammad Abdol-Mon'em Khafājī, professor at the al-Azhar seminary, writes about the personality of Imam Ja'far as-Sādeq ؏ in the introduction to his book *al-imām as-sādeq kamā 'orrafahu 'olamā al-gharb*: "When we speak of Imam Ja'far as-Sādeq ؏, we are speaking of the greatest and most influential person in the history of Islamic thought and civilization, with the highest and most excellent virtues and accomplishments, who has been seminal in the founding of different

legal and theological schools of thought. Praise Imam Ja'far as-Sādeq ﷺ and be not afraid! Speak of his lineage from the House of Prophethood and that he was the heir of the virtues and excellences and accomplishments and knowledge and wisdom of that noble House! Speak of his piety and asceticism and religiosity and devotion to God ﷻ! Speak of his knowledge of Islam and his juridical scholarship and the way in which he handled the political turmoil of his time and his righteous struggle with those difficulties, and his waging war with tyranny! Speak of his wise understanding of [the trials and tribulations of] life and his deep understanding of his era and his people, of his loving [service to] Islam, of his hatred of bloodshed; better yet, simply speak of every noble and praiseworthy characteristic which distinguishes the great men of history!"267

7. Imam Mūsā b. Ja'far al-Kāzem

The following is a selection of what Sunni scholarship has said about Imam Mūsā Kāzem ﷺ.

1. Abū-Hātam Rāzī Muhammad b. Edrīs (d. 277 AH), a great scholar of the science of hadīth, says that Imam Mūsā Kāzem ﷺ "was truthful, was a reliable and trustworthy authority [as a transmitter of hadīth] (*thaqa; wūthūq*), and was one of the leaders [of the community]."268

2. The great historian Ya'qūbī (d. 284 AH) says, "[Imam] Mūsā Kāzem ﷺ was one of the most devout people [within the community of the faithful]."269

3. Abol-Faraj Abdor-Rahmān b. Ali b. Muhammad b. Jowzī (d. 597 AH) has said, "[Imam] Mūsā Kāzem ﷺ was dedicated to the devotion and adoration of God ﷻ and was highly munificent. Whenever he heard news

of a person falling prey to iniquity, he would send a thousand dīnars to him and would visit him personally as a token of his friendship."²⁷⁰

4. Muḥammad b. Ṭalḥa ash-Shāfeʾī (d. 652 AH) says, "[Imam] Mūsā Kāzem ﷺ was a great leader of high standing. He was diligent in his ritual devotions and was famous for his dedication to the devotion and adoration of God ﷻ. There are [reports extant from] witnesses who have attested to his "impossible wonders" and extra-ordinary feats (*karāmāt*). He would spend his nights in prostration and standing in devotion, worship and supplication, and spend his days in fasting and alms-giving. He was called "al-Kāzem" (one who has forbearance) on account of his extreme forbearance and restraint. He would react to those who transgressed against him with good deeds, and would forgive criminals their transgressions. He was [also] called the Godly Devotee (*al-ʾabd aṣ-ṣāliḥ*) on account of the longevity of his devotions. In the ʿIrāq he was known as the *bāb ol-ḥawāʾej* (the door to [the fulfillment of] one's needs) toward [i.e. in attaining proximity to] God ﷻ, and this was because the needs of those who would seek intercessory recourse (*tawassol*)²⁷¹ with him would have their needs fulfilled. His "impossible wonders" and extra-ordinary feats (*karāmāt*) are bewildering and astonishing and speak to [Imam] Mūsā Kāzem's ﷺ having attained to the Station of Truth (*ṣedq*) with God ﷻ, [a station] which, [when reached by its recipient, means that his soul] neither falters nor is it annihilated."²⁷²

5. Sabṭ b. Jowzī (d. 654 AH) describes Imam Mūsā Kāzem ﷺ in the following terms: "He was known by the epithets al-Kāzem (the One who has Forbearance), al-Maʾmūn (the Secure Refuge), al-Ṭayyeb (the Pure), and as-Seyyed (the Master). His agnomen (*konya*) was Abol-Ḥasan and was called the Godly Devotee (*al-ʾabd aṣ-ṣāliḥ*) on account of the longevity of his devotions… [Imam] Mūsā Kāzem ﷺ had a generous and forbearing spirit. He was called "al-Kāzem" because whenever he heard

news of a person falling prey to hardship, he would send them some money."[273]

6. The renowned Shāfi'ī Mo'tazelī scholar Eben Abī'l-Hadīd (d. 656 AH) states: "[Imam] Mūsā Kāzem ﷺ was a righteous devotee [of God ﷻ] (*al-'abd as-sālih*). He combined in his person the scholarly understanding of religion, righteousness of conduct, religious devotion, patience, forbearance and perseverance."[274]

7. Hāfez Abol-Hajjāj al-Mazzī (d. 742 AH) and Dhahabī (d. 747 AH) relate: "[Imam] Mūsā Kāzem ﷺ was known as the godly Devotee (*al-'abd as-sālih*) because he used to spend his nights in worship and supplication and on account of the longevity of his devotions. It has been related by our associates that he entered the Mosque of the Prophet ﷺ [in Medina] and went into prostration at sunset and continued repeating [invocations and praises to God ﷻ in this position] until dawn. He was a munificent and generous man."[275]

8. Dhahabī (d. 747 AH) adds, "[Imam] Mūsā Kāzem ﷺ was a scholar and a God-fearing and righteous devotee of God ﷻ."[276]

9. The Yemenite historian and Sufi Abdollāh b. As'ad al-Yāfe'ī ash-Shāfe'ī (d. 767 AH) says, "Master Abol-Hasan Mūsā Kāzem ﷺ was the son of [Imam] Ja'far as-Sādeq ﷺ, and had an exalted stature [in the community]. He was dedicated to the devotion and adoration of God ﷻ (*'ābed*), was munificent, was forbearing, and is believed by the Imāmīya to be one of the twelve immaculate (*ma'sūm*) Imams. He was known as the Godly Devotee (*al-'abd as-sālih*) because of the frequency of his devotions and worship. He was a munificent and generous man.""[277]

10. The great biographer and Quranic exegete Eben Kathīr (d. 774 AH) states: "[Imam] Mūsā Kāzem ﷺ was dedicated to the devotion and adoration of God ﷻ. He was chivalrous and generous; whenever he heard news of a person falling prey to hardship, he would send them some money and gifts."[278]

11. Allāme Eben Sabbāgh al-Makkī (d. 855 AH), the leader of the Mālekī religio-legal rite (*madhhab*) of his era, writes about Imam Hasan as follows:

    11.1. "The virtues and evident "impossible wonders" and extra-ordinary feats (*karāmāt*) of [Imam] Mūsā Kāzem ﷺ testify that nobility originates, gathers in waves and reaches full flower in him. The steed of Nobleness and Grace kneels before him, allowing him to mount it and gallop at speed. He has command over all of the trophies of munificence and chooses the best for himself."[279]

    11.2. Eben Sabbāgh adds: "[Imam] Mūsā Kāzem ﷺ was the most devout and most knowledgeable and most munificent man of his generation. He would visit the indigent of Medina by [cover of] night and give them money and pensions, and they only became aware of who it was who supported them after he died."[280][281]

12. Muhammad Khāje-ye Pārsā-ye Bokhārī (d. 865 AH), the magister (*faqīh*), scholar of the science of hadīth, and Sūfī says, [Imam] Mūsā Kāzem ﷺ had an exalted stature [in the community of the faithful]. He was dedicated to the devotion and adoration of God ﷻ (*'ābed*), was munificent, was forbearing, and had a vast amount of knowledge. He was known as the godly Devotee (*al-'abd as-sālih*) because of the frequency of his devotions and worship; he is known to [have] enter[ed] into prostration to God ﷻ at sunrise and to remain in prostration until [the time of the] noon [ritual devotions, and some say he does this frequently and even] on a daily basis."[282]

3 The Evidence

13. Ahmad b. Hajar al-Haythamī al-Makkī (d. 974 AH) says, "[Imam] Mūsā Kāzem ﷺ was the heir and successor of his father in learning and the practical application of the teachings [of Islam] (*ma'refa'*) and in the acquisition and perfection of all virtues. He was called "al-Kāzem" (one who has forbearance) on account of his extreme forbearance and restraint. To the people of the 'Iraq he was known as the *bāb ol-hawā'ej* (the door to [the fulfillment of] one's needs) toward [i.e. in attaining proximity to] God ﷻ, [and this was because the needs of those who would seek intercessory recourse (*tawassol*)[283] with him would have their needs fulfilled]. [Imam] Mūsā Kāzem ﷺ was the most devout and most knowledgeable and most munificent man of his generation."[284]

14. The Egyptian Shāfe'ite scholar Muhammad b. Ali as-Sabbān (known as Eben Sabbān) (d. 1206 AH) says, "[Imam] Mūsā Kāzem ﷺ was known to the people of the 'Iraq as the *bāb ol-hawā'ej* (the door to [the fulfillment of] one's needs) toward [i.e. in attaining proximity to] God ﷻ, [and this was because the needs of those who would seek intercessory recourse (*tawassol*)[285] with him would have their needs fulfilled]. [Imam] Mūsā Kāzem ﷺ was the most devout man of his generation, and was one of its most knowledgeable scholars of religion."[286]

15. Shaykh Yūsof b. Esmāīl an-Nabhānī al-Beyrūtī (d. 1350 AH) who was the chief magistrate of Beirut says, "[Imam] Mūsā Kāzem ﷺ was one of the brightest [stars of the firmament] and greatest Imams from among our Masters, the *ahl al-bayt* ﷺ (the People of the House [of the Prophet ﷺ]). He was one [of the select] who was graced with "impossible wonders" and extra-ordinary feats (*karāmāt*) and is a Guide to [the true teachings of] Islam; may God ﷻ be pleased with them all and grant us of their blessings (*baraka'*), and sacrifice our souls for the cause of our love for them and for their [even] better ancestor, [the Prophet Muhammad ﷺ]."[287]

16. Shaykh Mostafā Rashdī (d. 1309 AH), the son of Shaykh Esmā'īl ad-Dameshqī, says, "Abū-Ebrāhīm Imam Mūsā Kāzem ﷺ would spend his nights in prostration and standing in devotion, worship and supplication, and his days in fasting and alms-giving. He was called "al-Kāzem" (one who has forbearance) on account of his extreme forbearance and restraint. He would react to those who transgressed against him with good deeds, and would forgive criminals their transgressions. He was [also] called the Godly Devotee (*al-'abd as-sālih*) on account of the longevity of his devotions. In the 'Iraq he was known as the *bāb ol-hawā'ej* (the door to [the fulfillment of] one's needs) toward [i.e. in attaining proximity to] God ﷻ, [and this was because the needs of those who would seek intercessory recourse (*tawassol*)[288] with him would have their needs fulfilled]. [Imam] Mūsā Kāzem's devotions and worship are legendary and speak to his having attained to the Station of Truth (*sedq*) with God ﷻ, [a station] which, [when reached by its recipient, means that his soul] neither falters nor is it annihilated. His "impossible wonders" and extraordinary feats (*karāmāt*) are astonishing and bewilder [hitherto sober] minds."[289]

17. Shaykh YāSīn b. Ebrāhīm as-Sanhūtī ash-Shāfe'ī says, "[Imam] Mūsā Kāzem, may God ﷻ be pleased with him, was a paragon of patience, forbearance, devout religiosity and piety. He overtook everyone in the arena of the ascendancy of [his] proximity [to God ﷻ] (*sīyādaʿ al-welāyaʿ*) and in the sovereignty of the nobility [i.e. of the *ahl al-bayt* ﷺ, the House of the Prophet ﷺ] (*welāyaʿ as-sīyādaʿ*). He was called "al-Kāzem" (one who has forbearance) on account of his extreme forbearance and restraint. He would react to those who transgressed against him with good deeds, and would forgive criminals their transgressions. In the 'Iraq he was known as the *bāb ol-hawā'ej* (the door to [the fulfillment of] one's needs) toward [i.e. in attaining proximity to] God ﷻ, and this was because the needs of those who would seek intercessory recourse

(*tawassol*)²⁹⁰ with him would have their needs fulfilled. He was [also] called the Godly Devotee (*al-'abd as-sālih*) on account of the longevity of his devotions. He was the most devout man of his generation."²⁹¹

18. The contemporary biographer Khayrod-Dīn Zarkalī (d. 1410 AH) writes, "[Imam] Mūsā Kāzem ﷺ was of the lineage of the Banī-Hāshem and was the most devout man of his generation. He was a great scholar and was known for his generosity and munificence."²⁹²

19. Shaykh Muhammad Abdor-Ra'ūf al-Manāwī (d. 1331 AH) says, "[Imam] Mūsā Kāzem ﷺ was one of the most devout men of his generation. He was a great scholar and was known for his generosity and munificence."²⁹³

20. Shaykh Hamdollāh al-Hendī al-Dājawī al-Hanafī says, "One of the proofs for the permissibility of seeking intercessory recourse (*tawassol*)²⁹⁴ after [the intermediary's] death is what imam Shāfe'ī has said, namely, that 'the grave of [Imam] Mūsā Kāzem ﷺ is a veritable panacea for the answer to one's prayers.'"²⁹⁵

8. Imam Ali b. Mūsā ar-Reḍā

The following is a selection of what Sunni scholarship has said about Imam Ali b. Mūsā ar-Reḍā ﷺ.

1. Hasan b. as-Sahl (d. 236 AH), the wily vizier of the Abbāsid caliph al-Ma'mūn and his father in law says, "Verily, al-Ma'mūn appointed [Imam] Ali b. Mūsā ar-Reḍā ﷺ as his heir-apparent because he could not find among the progeny of al-Abbās and the progeny of Ali anyone more preeminent, more pious, and more knowledgeable."²⁹⁶

2. Abū-Hātam Muhammad b. Hebbān (d. 354 AH) the great historian and prosopographer says, "[Imam] Ali b. Mūsā ar-Reḍā ﷺ was a dignitary from the *ahl al-bayt* ﷺ (the People of the House [of the Prophet ﷺ]), a man of letters from among that House and of the Banī-Hāshem²⁹⁷ [more generally], and he was their elder statesman. His grave is in Sanābād outside of Nūqān next to the grave of Hārūn or-Rashīd, and is a famous shrine and place of pilgrimage. I have made pilgrimage to it on numerous occasions. My prayers were answered every time without fail whenever I was in Tūs [the location of the shrine of Imām Reḍā ﷺ] and made a pilgrimage to the shrine of Imam Reḍā ﷺ in order [to ask him to intercede on my behalf] so that my troubles might be solved; and this I experienced on numerous occasions. May God ﷻ take our souls with the love of Mostafā (The Chosen One – a title of the Prophet) ﷺ and the love of his *ahl al-bayt* ﷺ in our hearts."²⁹⁸

3. Abū-Muhammad Abdollāh b. Muhammad al-Qadāma al-Moqaddasī (d. 620 AH), the great Hanbalī magister (*faqīh*) and author of the famous book *al-moghnī fī sharh al-kharqī* states, "Ja'far b. Muhammad as-Sādeq ﷺ and his son, Mūsā b. Ja'far al-Kāzem ﷺ and his son Ali b. Mūsā ar-Reḍā ﷺ are all imams with whom God ﷻ is contented, and their virtues are as abundant as they are famous."²⁹⁹

4. Muhammad b. Talha ash-Shāfe'ī says, "We talked about Ali, Amīr al-Mo'menīn ﷺ (the Commander of the Faithful) and Ali Zeyn ol-Ābedīn ﷺ (the Adornment of the Devotees), and now we come to the third Ali, Ali b. Mūsā ar-Reḍā ﷺ. Anyone who pays careful attention will find the latter to be the heir and successor of the first two. His faith grew and his [spiritual] station was lofty and expansive; his followers were numerous and [the veracity of] his case was evident. And this is why the Abbāsid caliph al-Ma'mūn made him a partner in the caliphate, gave him his daughter's hand in marriage, and made him his heir apparent. His virtues

and attributes are excellent, his munificence is like Hātam at-Tā'ī's,[300] his good nature is taken from his father, his etiquette and comportment are that of an Arab [dignitary], his noble soul is that of a Hāshemite, and his magnanimous lineage is that of the House of Prophethood. He is better than whatever can be said of the excellence of his virtues."[301]

5. The renowned Shāfe'ī Mo'tazelī scholar Eben Abī'l-Hadīd (d. 656 AH) states: "Ali b. Mūsā ar-Reḍā ﷺ was the most knowledgeable and most munificent man [of his generation]."[302]

6. Dhahabī (d. 747 AH) Says,
    6.1. "Ali b. Mūsā ar-Reḍā ﷺ had a high standing in scholarship, religiosity and nobility of lineage… He had a high rank and was worthy [of the office of] the caliphate."[303]
    6.2. He also says, "Ali b. Mūsā ar-Reḍā ﷺ was the Master of the Banī-Hāshem of his generation, and he was their best and brightest."[304]

7. The biographer Eben Hajar al-Asqalānī (d. 852 AH) and the genealogist Sam'ānī (d. 564 AH) say, "In addition to being endowed with the nobility of lineage, Ali b. Mūsā ar-Reḍā ﷺ was a virtuous scholar."[305]

8. Ahmad b. Hajar al-Heythamī al-Makkī (d. 974 AH) says, "Ali b. Mūsā ar-Reḍā ﷺ was the most renowned and the best of the Ahl al-Bayt ﷺ (the Members of the Household [of the Prophet] ﷺ). This is why the Abbāsid caliph al-Ma'mūn made him a partner in the caliphate, gave him his daughter's hand in marriage, and made him his heir apparent.

9. Shaykh Abdollāh b. Muhammad b. 'Āmer ash-Shabrāwī ash-Shāfe'ī (d. 1172 AH), the leading professor of the al-Azhar seminary of his time, says, "Ali b. Mūsā ar-Reḍā ﷺ is one of the Imams, may God ﷻ be pleased with him. He was endowed with dignity and grandeur and was generous

and illustrious. His father [Imam] Mūsā al-Kāzem ﷺ loved him very much."³⁰⁶

10. Shaykh Yūsof b. Esmā'īl an-Nabhānī (D. 1265 AH) says, "Ali b. Mūsā ar-Reḍā ﷺ was one of the greatest imams and brightest lights of the community [hailing] from the House of Prophethood. He was a veritable mine of knowledge, gnosis, magnanimity and chivalry. He was a great man of high standing and renown, and was gifted with "impossible wonders" and extra-ordinary feats (karāmāt)."³⁰⁷

11. The contemporary author Ali b. Muhammad b. Abdollāh al-Fekrī reports, "Ebrāhīm b. Abbās [as-Sūlī, one of the greatest poets of his generation] has said, 'Never was [Imam] Reḍā ﷺ asked a question to which he did not know the answer. I never knew anyone who was as aware of the events of history and [of events] up to the present day as Ali b. Mūsā ar-Reḍā ﷺ. [The Abbāsid] caliph al-Ma'mūn would quiz him on different subjects, and he always answered with perfect responses... He needed little sleep and fasted very often. He never fasted less than three days a month and would say that [the rewards for] these [extra-erogatory] fasts are [the equivalent to the bounties of] the entire world [in the world which is to come in the hereafter]. He gave profusely in charity and performed [other] good deeds, most of which he did [under cover of] the darkness of night.³⁰⁸ He was a legend of asceticism and God-fearing piety (war')."³⁰⁹

12. Abdol-Mot'al as-Sa'īdī al-Mesrī, professor of linguistics at the al-Azhar seminary, says, "[Imam Ali b. Mūsā ar-Reḍā ﷺ] had a high standing [as a consequence of his mastery of the Quranic] sciences, and [was an adept in the ways of] God-fearing piety (war')."³¹⁰

13. Shaykh YāSīn b. Ebrāhīm as-Sanhūtī ash-Shāfe'ī says, "God ﷻ made the precious existence of Imam Ali ar-Reḍā ﷺ as the highest symbol of His power [of creativity] ... He had a high standing [in the community], was famous for the excellence of his virtues, his mention was always accompanied with praise, and he was gifted with abundant "impossible wonders" and extra-ordinary feats (karāmāt)."[311]

9. Imam Muhammad b. Ali al-Jawād

The following is a selection of what Sunni scholarship has said about Imam Muhammad b. Ali al-Jawād ﷺ.

1. Muhammad b. Talha ash-Shāfe'ī (d. 652 AH) says, "Abū-Ja'far [Muhammad b. Ali (Imam al-Jawād) ﷺ] the second Muhammad... was renowned and had a high standing [in the community] despite his youth."[312]

2. Sabt b. Jowzī (d. 654 AH) describes Imam Jawād ﷺ in the following terms: "He followed in his father's footsteps in his knowledge, piety, asceticism and munificence."[313]

3. Shaykh ol-Islām Eben Teymīya (d. 728 AH) says "Muhammad b. Ali al-Jawād ﷺ was a dignitary of the Banī-Hāshem and was known for his eminence and generosity, which is why he was known as al-Jawād (the Munificent)."[314]

4. Shamsoddīn Muhammad b. Yūsof b. Hasan al-Ansārī az-Zarandī al-Madanī al-Hanafī (d. 747 AH) says, "Muhammad b. Ali al-Jawād ﷺ was an imam, a scholar, of sound character, was God-fearing, was devout, put [his beliefs] into practice, was an ascetic, was perfected, was courageous, was munificent, was pure, was reliable and trustworthy, was a guide to [religious] development and the acquisition of [the] honors

[which that path entails], and was the *walī* (1. regent, sovereign, lord and master; 2. patron, guardian, protector, custodian) [of the community of the faithful] and had the title of at-Taqī (the Pious)."³¹⁵

5. Ahmad b. Hajar al-Haythamī al-Makkī (d. 974 AH) reports, as have several other Sunni scholars: "The Abbāsid caliph al-Ma'mūn honored and was generous to Imam Jawād ﷺ; when he decided to give the hand of his daughter Omm Faḍl to Imam Jawād ﷺ in marriage, the Banī-Abbās clan grew concerned and tried to dissuade him from his decision. al-Ma'mūn explained the reason for his decision as [the extraordinary breadth of] the knowledge of the Imam, the excellence of his virtues, and his forbearance, all of which are greater than all of the other scholars, adepts and divines, despite the Imam's youth. The Banī-Abbās clan differed on this point and decided to settle the matter by putting the Imam ﷺ to the test. They thus ordered Yahyā b. Aktham, the great magister and scholar of the era to [appear in the court of] al-Ma'mūn, promising the latter that Yahyā b. Aktham would humiliate Imam Jawād ﷺ. And so it was arranged. They seated Imam Jawād ﷺ in a place of honor, and Yahyā b. Aktham proceeded to put his questions to the young Imam, who answered them all perfectly. al-Ma'mūn then turned to Imam Jawād ﷺ and told him that he had done well, and asked him if he, in his turn, had any questions for Yahyā b. Aktham? And so the Imam asked Yahya: 'What do you say about [the case of] a man who looks at a woman in an unlawful manner in the early morning, who then becomes lawful to him [to look at with carnal desire] before noon, and become unlawful to him [again] at noon, only to become lawful to him [yet again] in the afternoon, and becomes unlawful to him [for a third time] at sunset, who becomes lawful to him [for a third time] at the time of the night (*eshā*) ritual devotions (*salā*'), and becomes unlawful to him [for a fourth time] at midnight, and becomes lawful to him [for a fourth time] at daybreak?' Yahyā said, 'I do not know!' Imam Jawād ﷺ said, 'The

person [in question] is a slave-girl (*kanīz*) which a non-Arab (*ajnabī*) man looked upon with lust, which was unlawful to him; the man then buys the slave-girl before noon, only to free her at noon; he then marries her in the afternoon; and divorces (*zehār*)[316] her at sunset; [and regrets his action] and pays the atonement price (*kaffāra*) [of the *zehār* divorce], at night, [thereby making her lawful to him again]; at midnight, he makes a *raj'ī*[317] divorce with her, and "returns" to her at daybreak.' At this point, Ma'mūn turned to his kinfolk and exclaimed, 'Now do you see that which you were bent on denying?' He then married his daughter Omm Fadl to Imam Jawād ﷺ before the same assembly."[318] [319]

6. Khāja Abdolfattāh b. Muhammad an-No'mān al-Hanafi al-Hendī (d. 1096 AH) says, "The agnomen (*konya*) of Imam Muhammad b. Ali [Imam Jawād ﷺ] was Abū-Ja'far, so that he had the same agnomen as well as the same name as his ancestor [Abū-Ja'far Muhammad b. Ali] Imam al-Bāqer ﷺ, which is why they called him Abū-Ja'far the Second. He was gifted with "impossible wonders" (*karāmāt*) and extra-ordinary feats (*khawāreq*) from his [early] childhood."[320]

7. Shaykh Yūsof b. Esmā'īl an-Nabhānī (d. 1265 AH) says, "Muhammad al-Jawād b. Ali ﷺ was one of the great Imams and was a shining light of the community from our Lords and Masters (*sādātonā*), the *ahl al-bayt* ﷺ (the People of the House [of the Prophet ﷺ])."[321]

8. Dr. Abdossalām al-Termedhī says, "Abū-Ja'far, known as al-Jawād ﷺ, was the ninth Imam of the Imams of the Imāmīya (Twelver) *madhhab*. He was intelligent and had a capable tongue which had quick retorts at the ready (was quick-witted)."[322]

9. Khayroddīn az-Zarkalī says, "Muhammad b. Ali [al-Jawād ﷺ] was the ninth Imam of the Imams of the Imāmīya (Twelver) *madhhab*. Like his

father, he had a high standing in the community, was highly intelligent, had a capable tongue and was quick-witted."³²³

10. Ali al-Hosaynī al-Fakrī al-Qāheraī says, "[the Abbāsid caliph] al-Ma'mūn held Imam Jawād in high honor and esteem and was very generous to him, making him his advisor and confidante (*moqarrab*). He was enamored to him because of the excellences of his virtues, [the greatness of] his knowledge, the perfection of his mind and the unassailable logic [of his arguments]. He had decided to give the hand of his daughter Omm Faḍl to Imam Jawād ﷺ in marriage, but the Banī-Abbās clan grew concerned and tried to dissuade him from his decision because they feared that he would delegate the heir-apparancy to Imam Jawād ﷺ just as his father had given it to Imam Reḍā ."³²⁴

10. Imam Hasan b. Ali al-Hādī

The following is a selection of what Sunni scholarship has said about Imam Ali b. Muhammad al-Hādī.

1. Muhammad b. Talha ash-Shāfe'ī (d. 652 AH) says, "The virtues of Abol-Hasan Ali b. Muhammad [Imam al-Hādī ﷺ] have taken their position in the ears [of the wise] like the gemstones of earrings, and just as a pair of shells envelope and protect their valuable pearl, the ears too embrace the excellence of his virtues with fascination; virtues which testify to the fact that the soul of Abol-Hasan [Imam al-Hādī ﷺ] is endowed with the purest of attributes and that it has descended from the Station of Prophethood unto the Sons of the Nobility."³²⁵

2. The great biographer and Quranic exegete Eben Kathīr (d. 774 AH) states: "Abol-Hasan Ali [Imam al-Hādī ﷺ] was dedicated to the devotion and adoration of God ﷻ (*'ābed*) and lead a simple ascetic life."³²⁶

3. Muhammad Khāje-ye Pārsā-ye Bokhārī (d. 865 AH), the magister (*faqīh*), scholar of the science of hadīth, and Sūfī says, "Abol-Hasan Ali [Imam al-Hādī 🕮] was dedicated to the devotion and adoration of God 🕮 (*ābed*), was a magister (i.e. a scholar of the religious sciences: a *faqīh*), and an imam (leader of the faithful)."³²⁷

4. Ahmad b. Hajar al-Haythamī al-Makkī (d. 974 AH) says, "Abol-Hasan Ali [Imam al-Hādī 🕮] was the heir to his father in terms of [the extent of] his knowledge and learning, and in terms of his munificence and largess."³²⁸

5. Abol-Faraj Abdol-Hayy b. 'Amād al-Hanbalī (d. 1089 AH) says, "Abol-Hasan Ali [Imam al-Hādī 🕮] was a magister (*faqīh*), was an *imam* (leader of the faithful), and was dedicated to the devotion and adoration of God 🕮 (*ābed*)."³²⁹

6. Khayroddīn az-Zarkalī says, "Abol-Hasan Ali b. Muhammad known as al-Hādī 🕮 ... was righteous and God-fearing."³³⁰

7. Ali al-Hosaynī al-Fakrī al-Qāheraī says, "Abol-Hasan al-Askarī [al-Hādī 🕮] was the heir and successor of his father in terms of [the extent of] his knowledge and learning, and in terms of his munificence and largess." He was a magister (*faqīh*), was eloquent, elegant and dignified. He was the most genial and most truthful of people."³³¹

11. Imam Hasan b. Muhammad al-Askarī

The following is a selection of what Sunni scholarship has said about Imam Hasan b. Muhammad al-Askarī 🕮.

1. Sabt b. Jowzī (d. 654 AH) describes Imam Hasan b. Muhammad al-Askarī ﷺ in the following terms: "He was a scholar and a reliable and trustworthy [transmitter of hadīth] (*thiqa*)."³³²

2. Khayroddīn az-Zarkalī says, "Imam Hasan b. Muhammad al-Askarī ﷺ followed in the footsteps of his righteous forefathers in his piety and dedication to the devotion and adoration of God ﷻ."³³³

The rest of the scholars from within the Sunni community have similar words of praise for the Imams of the Shī'a, either individually or as a whole, the details of which we will refrain from, referring the reader instead to their authoritative sources. Examples of these include the following: Eben Jowzī, *Tadhketa' an-Khawās*; Eben Sabbāq, *al-Fūsūl al-Mohemma*; Tabarī, *Dhakhāer al-'Oqbā*; Eben Tūtūn, *al-A'emma' al-Ethnā'ashar*; Dhahabī, *Tadhkera' al-Hoffāz*; Ansārī, *al-Jowhara fi nasab al-imām 'alī wa ālahū*; Eben Kathīr, *al-Bidāya wa'n-Nahāya*; Ahmad b. Abī-Ya'qūb, *at-Tārīkh al-Ya'qūbī*; Eben Sa'd, *at-Tabaqāt al-Kobrā*; Eben Asāker, *at-Tārīkh al-Madīna' ad-Dameshq*; Qondūzī, *Yanābi' al-Mowadda*, etc.

4 Concluding Remarks

Taking the contents of the foregoing chapters into account, there can be no doubt that the fulfillment of the prophecy of the "Twelve Princes" from the seed of Ishmael concerning whom glad tidings are given in the Holy Bible, and whom the Prophet ﷺ had also prophesied would be his successors (*khalīfa*) (as testified to by hadīth reports which are to be found with impeccable provenance titles in all the authoritative Sunni sources), are none other than the Twelve Imams of the Twelver Shīʿa. They are linked together in one uninterrupted chain and who stand, as admitted by almost all of their enemies (let alone their friends), to have been at the height of the theoretical and practical wisdom of each of their respective generations. This is because they comprise the only collection of twelve great learned and pious personages in which the number twelve plays a significant role, and who have the special attribute (i.e. their brotherly or filial (father to son) relationship) which makes their number equal to no more and no less than twelve and which therefore separates them from the false contenders for the fulfillment of this prophecy.

In addition to the collection of twelve great personages who stand at the height of the theoretical and practical wisdom of each of their respective generations and who are linked together in one uninterrupted chain, the greatness and munificence of which has been stipulated by their enemies – despite their various motivations for hiding these virtues – the coming together of this constellation is an extraordinary phenomenon in the history of humanity – a phenomenon for which no precedent can be found in the histories of any race or nation. This is a divine miracle for those endowed with wisdom and understanding to see, and a manifest sign of the veracity and truthfulness of the path of these great men, and of their connection to the Invisible World (the world that is beyond the ken of ordinary human perception).

The other conclusion that can be drawn from the reports of the views of Sunnite scholarship concerning the Imams of the Shī'a is that the relationship which these Imams had with the ordinary folk and the scholars of the Sunni community was highly cordial and magnanimous. The Imams lived in the midst of the Sunni community, and the two socialized with each other, gave their sons and daughters in marriage to each other, accompanied each other on long journeys, and the Imams would even mentor them and relay to them hadīth reports from their ancestor, the Prophet ﷺ of Islam. The Imams dealt with the Sunni majority in such a way as to make the community think of the Ahl al-Bayt ؑ (the Imams of the House of Prophethood ﷺ) as one of them and as members of their community, just as their followers (Shī'a) thought of these great dignitaries as one of themselves. This behavior of theirs resulted in nothing but profuse love on the part of the masses and on the part of their scholars for the noble Imams. It was for this reason and on account of their countless virtues that a large number of the Sunni community honored them and held them in high esteem, despite the fact that they considered their partisans, the Shī'a, to have deviated and strayed and had become wayward. It goes without saying that had the Imams of the

4 Concluding Remarks

Shīʿa not had the kind of exemplary conduct that they were blessed with and stood their ground and insisted on their beliefs and what they believed to be their rights in a zealous and intolerant way, and secluded themselves from the generally Sunni society at large, and treated them with disrespect and contempt, turning themselves into the leaders of a minority sect, they would never have been the beneficiaries and objects of the love, honor and respect of Sunni scholarship and of the Sunni masses.

The manner of the Imams' conduct with respect to the Sunni community is a proof of this important and instructive point that these great men refrained from and avoided any sectarian behavior and mitigated any dynamic that would turn the group of their followers into a sect which was posed in opposition to the Sunnite majority which became grounds for divisiveness and disunity among the community of Muslims. Although they were adamant and insisted on the rightfulness of their beliefs and the beliefs of their Shīʿa, they were in no wise intent on founding a "sect" (*madhhab*) within the Sunni community, and were rather intent on preventing division from increasing into rancor, enmity and sectarian conflict. Their aim was no more and no less than acting as guides for the people to the true meanings and implications of the Quran and the prophetic *sonnaʿ* (exemplary model of conduct) and to correct the de facto deviations that had occurred in the community of faith in a way that was empathetic, compassionate and brotherly.

It would seem that the division of Muslim society into the two sects of Shīʿa and Sunni (and all of the consequent sectarian division in socialization, mosques, schools, neighborhoods, rites and rituals, etc.) is not what the Apostle ﷺ of God ﷻ the Exalted or his *ahl al-bayt* ﷺ (the Imams of his House) desired.

Today it is clear that following the admirable manner[334] of the *ahl al-bayt* who are the heritage of the Most Noble Prophet and are the second "Weighty Trust" beside the Noble Quran and are the "way of guidance and of avoiding error and misdirection,"[335] is a religious obligation (*wājeb*) incumbent on all Muslims, Shī'a and Sunni alike, and evasion of this divine ordinance (*farīḍa*) results in nothing other than the fanning of the fires of division and the continuation of ancient enmities and the murder of Muslims at the hands of other Muslims which is a disaster in which the Islamic community has become ensnared.

Today, nobody is more saddened and distraught at the short-sighted zealotry and fanaticism of some of us ignorant Muslims than the Apostle of God the Exalted and the People of his House, the *ahl al-bayt*. Today, the community of faith which the Apostle of God the Exalted founded with the help and sacrifice of his righteous and selfless Companions (may God be pleased with them) with untold hardship and against impossible odds, and which has been secured, nurtured and maintained by the People of his House, the Ahl al-Bayt together with the divinely-inspired scholars of the religion, has now fallen victim to ignorance (*jāhelīya'*) and fanaticism; and we are daily witness to the shedding of innocent Muslim blood at the hands of ignorant fanatics.

O my Cherishing and Nurturing and Guiding Lord (*yā rabb*)! Do not spare us Muslims from Your Guidance!

Amen.
Mas'ūd Emāmī
April 2016

4 Concluding Remarks

[Translator's note: The references and bibliography of the sources has been left untranslated because very few, if any, of these sources are available in English for non-Arabic speakers to refer to in any case. However, all of the sources are taken exclusively from the authoritative works from within Sunni scholarship. A sampling of the sources referred to (whose names have been "Romanized" for those English speakers who are interested to see who they are) has also been made available (in addition to the bibliography in Arabic), and this has been provided at the beginning of the bibliography section.]

Bibliography

(A sampling of the full bibliography is provided here in English)

Abī-Ya'lā, *Masnad*,
Abu-Dāwud, *as-Sonan*,
Abū-Zahra, *Tārīkh al-Madhāheb al-Islāmīya*
Ahmad b. Hanbal, *Masnad*
Beyhaqī, *Sonan*
Bokhārī, *Sahīh*
Dāramī, *Sonan*
Dhahabī, *Tārīkh al-Islam*
Eben Abī'l-Hadīd, Abdol-Hamīd, *Sharh-e Nahj ol-Balāgha*
Eben Abī-Shaybe
Eben Asāker, *at-Tārīkh al-Madīna' ad-Dameshq*
Eben Hajar, as-*Sawā'eq ol-Mahraqa*
Eben Hajr al-Asqalānī, *Fath ol-Bārī*
Eben Jowzī, *Tazkerat ol-Khawās*
Eben Kathīr, *at-Tārīkh*
Eben Khallakān, *Wafyāt al-'Ayān*
Eben Māja, *Sonan*
Eben Sabbāq al-Mālekī, *al-Fosūl al-Mohemma*
Eben-Sa'd, *Tabaqāt al-Kobrā*

Bibliography

Eben Taymīya, *Menhāj as-Sonna' an-Nabawīya*
Esfahānī, Ahmad b. Abdollāh, Abū-No'aym, *Helīat ol-Owlīā*
Hākem al-Haskānī an-Neyshāpurī, *al-Mostadrak 'Alā's-Sahīhayn*
Heythamī, *Majma' oz-Zawāed*
Khatīb al-Baghdādī, *Tarīkh al-Baghdād*
Muslim, *Sahīh*
Nasāī, *Khasāes al-Amīr al-Mo'menīn*
Qondūzī, *Yanabī al-Mawadda*
Rāzī, Fakhroddīn, *at-Tafsīr al-Kabīr*
Rāzī, Fakhroddīn, *Fusul al-Muhimmah*
Soyutī, *Dorr ol-Manthur*
Tabarī, *Tafsīr*
Tabarī, *Tārīkh ar-Rosol wa'l-Molūk*
Tayālasī, *Masnad*
Termedhī, *Jame'*
Wāqedī, *al-Moghāzī*
Ya'qūbī, *at-Tārīkh*

Endnotes

[1] Evidentialism is a thesis about epistemic justification; it is a thesis about what it takes for one to believe justifiably, or reasonably, in the sense thought to be necessary for knowledge.

[2] Conclusions which are deduced, interpolated or extrapolated from premises which are known with certainty.

[3] As-Sadr, Seyyed Muhammad Bāqer, *al-Fatāwā al-Wāḍiha*, p.19.

[4] *Fetric:* having to do with one's primordial disposition. Having to do with man's primordial nature and orientation; with the way in which man has been created.

[5] Plural form of *āya* or individual unit of revelation, often translated loosely as 'verse'.

[6] Author's note: Note the position of this *āya* and that it follows the one quoted earlier (41:52). The significance of the arrangement of these two *āyas* is that, based on the content of the first *āya*, someone who is in doubt about his faith must not allow his skepticism to act as an excuse to prevent him from taking a position on the most important religious principles, including the belief in God ﷻ. Thus, one can choose an option in which one has not attained to certainty, and according to the substance of this *āya*, the way to arrive at a choice of a preferred (though uncertain) option over other less certain potions is through an analysis of the evidence and indicators which are at hand. In other words, the position of these two *āyas* in immediate succession is an expression of the evidentialist methodology.

[7] Koleynī, *al-Kāfī*, 1:75 [of the Arabic edition].

[8] Abū-Hāmid Ghazālī, *The Revival of the Religious Sciences*, 4:61 [of the Persian edition].

[9] The New International Version (NIV) substitutes "rulers" for "princes", but most versions retain "princes".

[10] i.e. in Mecca.

[11] Genesis 25:14-17.

[12] Genesis 1:1-17

[13] Genesis 34:14-17

[14] The reference here is to the authoritative compilations of *hadīth* reports. *Hadīth*: A report of a saying or deed of the Prophet (or one of the Imāms, in the case of the Shī'a). The Prophet (and the Imāms in Shī'ā Islam) being embodied revelation, reports of their words and deeds comprise a body of scripture that is complementary to the Quran.

[15] Muslim, *Al-Sahih*, Part 6, p. 3; Al-Bukhari, *Al-Sahih*, C8, p. 127; Ahmed bin Hanbal, *Al-Musnad*, vol. 5, p. 86; Abi Dawood, *Al-Sunan*, Part 2, p.309; Al-Tirmidhi, *Al-Sunan*, vol. 3, p. 34; Nishapuri, Mustadrak Al-Sahihaynn, Part 3, p. 617; Al-Haythami, *Majma 'Al-Zawaid*, Part 5, p. 191; Al-Tayalisi, *Al-Musnad*, p. 105; Ibn Jaad, *Al-Musnad*, p. 390; Al-Tabarani, *Al-Mujam al-Kabir*, Part 2, p. 195; Al-Muttaqi Al-Hindi, *Kanz ol-'āmāl*, Part 12, p. 32

[16] Mar'ashī an-Najafī, *Sharh Ahqāq ol-Haqq* المرعشى، موسوعة الامامة فى نصوص اهل السنة، ج5، ص 351 تا 392.

[17] الصدوق، عيون اخبار الرضا عليه‌السلام، ج2، ص54؛ الصدوق، الخصال، ص466؛ الصدوق، الامالى، ص387؛ الخزاز، كفاية الاثر، ص49؛ الطوسى، الغيبة، ص128، الجوهرى، مقتضب الاثر، ص4. (Sheikh Saddūq, *Oyūn Akhbār ar-Reḍā*; Kisāl, Amalī; Tūsī, *al-Ghayba*; etc.)

[18] ابن كثير، البداية و النهاية، ج1، ص Eben Kathīr 153؛ ج6، ص250؛ المقريزى، امتاع الاسماع، ج12، ص Eben Khaldūn, *Moqaddame*:306 ابن خلدون، تاريخ ابن خلدون، ج1، ص406؛ الذهبى، تاريخ الاسلام، ج3، ص Dhahabī, *Tārīkh al-Islam* 479؛ Beyhaqī البيهقى، دلائل النبوة، ج6، ص Eben Hajr al-Asqalānī, 523؛ النووى، شرح صحيح مسلم، ج12، ص201، ابن حجر، فتح البارى، ج13، ص *Fath ol-Bārī*, 182؛ المباركفورى، تحفة الاحوذى، ج6، ص391؛ عظيم آبادى، عون المعبود، ج11، ص244، المناوى، فيض القدير، ج2، ص582؛ ابورية، اضواء على السنة المحمدية، ص233.

[19] شوشترى، نورالله، الصوارم المهرقة، ص93؛ المظفر، دلائل الصدق، ج6، ص264، Sayyed Askari, عسكرى، سيد مرتضى، معالم المدرستين، ج1، ص Mortadā, *Moālem ol-Madresatayn* 333؛ سبحانى، جعفر، الالهيات، ج4، ص Sobhānī, Ja'far; 111؛ الفضلى، دروس فى اصول الفقه الاماميه، ص181؛ فقيه ايمانى، الامام على عليه‌السلام فى آراء الخلفاء، ص14.

[20] One of the greatest poets of the Persian language. 14th Century.

[21] Eleven rather than twelve because it will be recalled that the twelfth imam went into a state of occultation or physical seclusion in the year 329 AH or 940 of the Christian era.

22 - Eben Asāker, at-Tārīkh al-Madīna' ad-Dameshq, ابن عساكر، تاريخ مدينة دمشق، ج54، ص276: «عن أبى الزبير قال كنا عند جابر بن عبدالله و قد كف بصره و علت سنه فدخل عليه على بن الحسين و معه ابنه محمد وهو صبى صغير فسلم على جابر و جلس فقال لابنه محمد قم إلى عمك فك عليه و قبل رأسه ففعل الصبى ذلك فقال جابر من هذا فقال محمد ابنى فضمه إليه و بكى وقال يا محمد إن رسول الله (صلى الله عليه وسلم) يقرأ عليك السلام فقال له صحبه و ما ذاك أصلحك الله فقال كنت عند رسول الله (صلى الله عليه وسلم) فدخل عليه الحسين بن على فضمّه إليه وقبّله و أقعده إلى جنبه ثم قال يولد لابنى هذا ابن يقال له على إذا كان يوم القيامة نادى مناد من بطنان العرش ليقم سيد العابدين فيقوم هو و يولد له محمد إذا رأيته يا جابر فاقرأ منى عليه السلام واعلم أن بقاءك بعد ذلك اليوم قليل فما لبث جابر بعد ذلك اليوم إلا بضعةَ عشر يوما حتى توفى». همچنين: همان، ج41، ص370؛ Dhahabī, Mīzān al-I'tedāl الذهبى، ميزان الاعتدال، ج3، ص550؛ Eben Hajar, Lisān al-Mīzān ابن حجر، لسان الميزان، ج5، ص168؛ -Eben Kathīr, al Badāya wa'l-Nahāya ابن كثير، البداية و النهاية، ج9، ص124. آيت الله مرعشى نجفى اين روايت را از سيزده منبع اهل سنت غير از منابع ذكر شده نقل كرده است، مراجعه شود به: المرعشى النجفى، احقاق الحق، ج12، ص13.

23 - Dhahabī, Seyr-e E'lām ol-Anbīā الذهبى، سير اعلام النبلاء، ج4، ص404: «ابن عقدة: حدثنا محمد بن عبدالله بن أبى نجيح، حدثنا على بن حسان القرشى، عن عمه عبدالرحمن بن كثير، عن جعفر بن محمد، قال: قال أبى: أجلسنى جدى الحسين فى حجره، و قال لى: رسول الله صلى الله عليه وسلم يقرئنك السلام. عن أبان بن تغلب، عن محمد بن على، قال: أتانى جابر بن عبدالله، و أنا فى الكتاب، فقال لى: اكشف عن بطنك، فكشفت، فألصق بطنه ببطنى، ثم قال: أمرنى رسول الله أن أقرئنك منه السلام.

24 - Tastarī, Ehqāq ol-Haqq التسترى، إحقاق الحق، ج12، ص352: «العلامة السيد على بن شهاب الدين الهمدانى فى (مودة القربى) (ص 140ط لاهور) روى عن عائشة قال (ص): من زار ولدى بطوس فإنما حج مرة قالت: مرةً فقال: مرتين، قالت: مرتين، فقال: ثلاث مرات فسكتت عائشة، فقال: ولو لم تسكتى لبلغت إلى سبعين. رأى رجل من أهل خراسان رسول الله (ص) يقول: كيف أنتم إذا دفن فى أرضكم بعضى فحكاها له (ع) فقال: أنا المدفون بأرضكم، ثم ذكر ثواب من زاره».

25 AH denotes *anno hegira qamaria*, or the Islamic calendar based on the lunar cycles.

26 - العجلى، معرفة الثقات، ج1، ص270.

27 - التسترى، إحقاق الحق، ج12، ص352 به نقل از «محاضرات الأدباء» (طبع بيروت) نوشته راغب اصفهانى، ج1، ص332.

28 Reference to a saying of the Prophet ﷺ concerning them.

29 It seems Shaykh Dhahabī has forgotten that Imam Hasan did indeed attain to the office of the caliphate, and was given pledges of allegiance by a greater number of people than that of the number of those who pledged their

allegiance to his august father, Imām Ali ﷺ, because the whole of Medīna pledged their allegiance to Imam Hasan ﷺ while some people demurred from doing so in the case of his father.

30 Fatwa: an authoritative legal opinion or ruling.

31 - Dhahabī, *Seyr E'lām ol-Anbīyā* الذهبی، سیر أعلام النبلاء، ج13، ص119.

32 - Eben Abī'l-Hadīd, Abdol-Hamīd, *Sharh-e Nahj ol-Balāgha* ابن ابی الحدید، شرح نهج البلاغه، ج15، ص278.

33 The House of the Prophet ﷺ and of Imām Ali b. Abī-Tāleb ﷺ.

34 Centered on or descended from Ali b. Abī-Tāleb ﷺ.

35 - Tastarī, *Ehqāq ol-Haqq* التستری، إحقاق الحق، ج19، ص621 به نقل از «الاتحاف بحب الأشراف» (طبع مصطفی البابی الحلبی، مصر)، نوشته عبدالله بن محمد شبراوی، ص68.

36 - Tastarī, *Ehqāq ol-Haqq* التستری، إحقاق الحق، ج28، ص446، به نقل از «المیراث عند الجعفریة» (طبع دار الرائد العربی، بیروت)، نوشته محمد ابو زهرة، ص34.

37 - Tastarī, *Ehqāq ol-Haqq* التستری، إحقاق الحق، ج28، ص293 به نقل از «تراجم الرجال» (طبع المطبعة التعاونیة)، نوشته محمد خضر حسین، ص29.

38 - Tastarī, *Ehqāq ol-Haqq* التستری، إحقاق الحق، ج19، ص621 به نقل از «ضوء الشمس» (طبع استانبول) نوشته محمد أبو الهدی الرفاعی، ج1، ص119.

39 - مرحوم آیت الله سید شهاب الدین مرعشی نجفی در ملحقات احقاق الحق به جمع آوری سخنان دهها دانشمند اهل سنت و منابع نخستین تا زمان حاضر درباره دوازده امام شیعیان پرداخته و مجلدات متعددی از کتاب خود را به این موضوع اختصاص داده است. این مجموعه گرانقدر یکی از منابع مهم کتاب حاضر بوده است.

(Footnote 39 cont'd) The author refers to the works of Āyatollāh Seyyed Shehāboddīn Mar‹ashī Najafī, who has taken strides in this direction, and acknowledges his work as a major reference source for this present book.

40 Another title for the fourth Imam meaning 'the prostrator' or 'the one who spends much time in prostration [to God]'.

41 The *tābe'īn* are the generation who followed the generation of the Associates (usually rendered as the Companions) of the Prophet ﷺ; in other words, those who were not themselves eye witnesses to the presence of the Prophet ﷺ but who personally witnessed one or more of his Associates.

42 The garrison later grew into a town and is now called Sāmarrā.

43 The Rashidun Caliphs (meaning "Rightly Guided"), often simply called, collectively, "the Rashidun", is a term used in Sunni Islam to refer to the 30-

year reign of the first four caliphs (successors) following the death of the prophet Muhammad ﷺ, namely: Abu Bakr, Umar, Uthman ibn Affan and Ali of the Rashidun Caliphate, the first caliphate. The concept of "Rightly Guided Caliphs" originated with the later Abbasid Caliphate based in Baghdad. It is a reference to the Sunni imperative "Hold firmly to my example (sunnah) and that of the Rightly Guided Caliphs" (Ibn Majah, Abu Dawood). They are called "Rightly Guided" because they have been seen as model Muslim leaders by Sunni Muslims.

44. Eben Kathīr, *al-Badāya wa'l-Nahāya* ابن كثير، البداية والنهاية، ج8، ص17؛ Eben Abdol-Barr ابن عبد البر، جامع بيان العلم و فضله، ج2، ص183.

45 The first generation after the generation of the Associates (*sahāba*).

46. Eben Abdol-Barr, *al-Estī'āb* ابن عبد البر، الاستيعاب، ج3، ص1117 – 1118؛ البرى، الجوهرة فى نسب الإمام على و آله، ص93 – 95؛ الصفدى، الوافى بالوفيات، ج21، ص180 – 18؛ Eben Asāker, *at-Tārīkh al-Madīna' ad-Dameshq* ابن عساكر، تاريخ مدينة دمشق، ج51 ص316؛

47 As opposed to the Ash‧arite or Māturīdites.

48. Ījī الايجى، المواقف، ج3، ص622؛ Jorjānī الجرجانى، شرح المواقف، ج8، ص365 – 366؛ Eben Hātam ابن حاتم، الدر النظيم، ص259؛ Dahabī, *Tārīkh al-Islām* الذهبى، تاريخ الإسلام، ج27، ص82 – 83؛ Eben Hajar, *Lisān al-Mīzān* ابن حجر، لسان الميزان، ج4، ص248؛

49. Tabarī, *Tārīkh ar-Rosol wa'l-Molūk*, الطبرى، تاريخ الطبرى، ج7، ص188؛ Eben Athīr, *al-Kāmel fi't-Tārīkh* ابن الأثير، الكامل فى التاريخ، ج6، ص408.

50. Eben Abī'l-Hadīd, Abdol-Hamīd, *Sharh-e Nahj ol-Balāgha* . ابن أبى الحديد، شرح نهج البلاغة، ج1، ص140.

51. Nasāī, *Khasāes al-Amīr al-Mo'menīn* خصائص امير المومنين على بن ابى طالب» نوشته احمد بن شعيب نسائى شافعى (م 303 ق)، «فضائل امير المومنين» نوشته ابن عقده كوفى (م 333 ق)، «النور المشتعل من كتاب ما نزل من القرآن فى على» نوشته احمد بن عبدالله بن احمد (م 430 ق) معروف به ابو نعيم اصفهانى، «مناقب على بن ابى طالب» نوشته على بن محمد بن محمد واسطى جُلّابى شافعى (م 483 ق) مشهور به ابن مغازلى، «المناقب» نوشته موفق بن احمد بن محمد حنفى خوارزمى (م 568 ق)، «جواهر المطالب فى مناقب الامام على بن ابى طالب» نوشته ابى البركات محمد بن احمد دمشقى باعونى شافعى (م 871 ق)، «سيرة الامام على بن ابى طالب» نوشته احمد بن عبدالله بكرى (م 891 ق)، «الامام على» نوشته عبد الفتاح عبد المقصود، «ترجمة على بن أبي طالب» نوشته أحمد زكى صفوة، «عبقرية الامام» نوشته عباس محمود العقاد، «على بن أبى طالب» نوشته حنا نمر، «على بن أبى طالب» در مجموعه الروائع نوشته فؤاد افرام بستانى، «على بن أبى طالب»، نوشته محمد سليم جندى،

Endnotes

52. «حیاة علی بن أبی طالب» نوشته محمد حبیب الله شنقیطی، «علی و بنوه» نوشته طه حسین، «علی إمام المتقین» نوشته عبدالرحمن شرقاوی، «صوت العدالة الإنسانیة» نوشته جرج جرداق نویسنده مسیحی، «الإمام علی بن أبی طالب کرم الله وجهه رابع الخلفاء الراشدین» نوشته محمد رضا، «الإمام علی بن أبی طالب» نوشته توفیق أبو علم، «الإمام علی نبراس و متراس» نوشته سلیمان کتانی نویسنده مسیحی و «حیاة الإمام علی» نوشته محمود شلبی. Eben Asāker, *at-Tārīkh al-Madīna' ad-Dameshq*، ابن عساکر، تاریخ مدینة دمشق، ذ ج42، ص411.

53. as-Safdī, *al-Wāfī bi'l-Wafyāt* - الصفدی، الوافی بالوفیات، ج21، ص179 - 180؛ ابن قتیبة، تأویل مختلف الحدیث، ص152؛ Eben Abdol-Barr, *al-Estī'āb* ابن عبد البر، الاستیعاب، ج3، ص1103؛ Eben Abī'l-Hadīd, Abdol-Hamīd, *Sharh-e Nahj ol-Balāgha* ابن أبی الحدید، شرح نهج البلاغة، ج1، ص16 - 23؛ Manāwī, *Fayḍ ol-Ghadīr* المناوی، فیض القدیر شرح الجامع الصغیر، ج4، ص470؛ المغربی، فتح الملک العلی، ص71.

54. Hākem al-Haskānī an-Neyshāpurī, *Shawāhed ot-Tanzīl* الحسکانی، شواهد التنزیل، ج1، ص34.

55. as-Safdī, *al-Wāfī bi'l-*Wafyāt الصفدی، الوافی بالوفیات، ج21، ص179 - 180؛ الذهبی، تاریخ الإسلام، ج3، ص637 - 638؛ Tabarī, *Tārīkh* الطبری، ذخائر العقبی، ص83؛ Eben Abdol-Barr, *al-Estī'āb* ابن عبد البر، الاستیعاب، ج3، ص1102.

56. Eben Qotayba, *Ta'wīl Mokhtalef al-Hadīth* ابن قتیبة، تأویل مختلف الحدیث، ص152؛ Eben Abī'l-Hadīd, Abdol-Hamīd, *Sharh-e Nahj ol-Balāgha* ابن أبی الحدید، شرح نهج البلاغة، ج1 ص16 - 23؛ Manāwī, *Fayḍ ol-Ghadīr* المناوی، فیض القدیر، ج4 ص470؛ Eben Asāker, *at-Tārīkh al-Madīna' ad-Dameshq* ابن عساکر، تاریخ مدینة دمشق، ج42، ص 405 - 406؛ المغربی، فتح الملک العلی، ص71؛ Eben Athīr, *Osod ol-Ghāba* ابن الأثیر، أسد الغابة، ج4، ص22.

57. Hākem al-Haskānī an-Neyshāpurī, *al-Mostadrak 'Alā's-Sahīhayn* النیشابوری، المستدرک، ج1، ص 457 - 458؛ العینی، عمدة القاری، ج9، ص240؛ Mottaqī al-Hendī, *Kanz ol-A'mmāl* الهندی، کنز العمال، ج5 ص 177 - 178؛ Manāwī, *Fayḍ ol-Ghadīr* المناوی، فیض القدیر، ج4، ص470؛ Soyutī, *ad-Dorr ol-Manthūr* السیوطی، الدر المنثور، ج3، ص144؛ الآلوسی، تفسیر الآلوسی، ج9، ص 108 - 109؛ Eben Asāker, *at-Tārīkh al-Madīna' ad-Dameshq* ابن عساکر، تاریخ مدینة دمشق، ج42، ص 405 - 406؛ Eben Borhān ash-Shāfe'ī, *as-Sīra' al-Halabīa* الحلبی، السیرة الحلبیة، ج1، ص 257 - 258.

58 الحسكانى، شواهد التنزيل، ج1، ص34. Hākem al-Haskānī an-Neyshāpurī, *Shawāhed ot-Tanzīl*

59 Soyutī. لسيوطى، الإتقان فى علوم القرآن، ج2، ص493؛ Eben Asāker, *at-Tārīkh al-Madīnaʿ ad-Dameshq* ابن عساكر، تاريخ مدينة دمشق، ج42، ص400؛ حاجى خليفة، كشف الظنون، ج1، ص429؛ المغربى، فتح الملك العلى، ص71.

60 Eben Qotayba, *al-Imama wa'l-Siyasa* ابن قتيبة، الامامة و السياسة، ج1، ص129.

61 Ya'qūbī, *at-Tārīkh* اليعقوبى، تاريخ اليعقوبى، ج2، ص187.

62 Bokhārī, *Tārīkh ak-Kabīr* البخارى، التاريخ الكبير، ج2، ص228 و 255؛ Eben Asāker, *at-Tārīkh al-Madīnaʿ ad-Dameshq* ابن عساكر، تاريخ مدينة دمشق، ج42، ص408؛ Safdī, *al-Wāfī bi'l-Wafyāt* الصفدى، الوافى بالوفيات، ج21، ص179 – 180؛ Dhahabī, *Tārīkh al-Islam* الذهبى، تاريخ الإسلام، ج3، ص637 – 638؛ Mottaqī al-Hendī, *Kanz ol-A'mmāl* المتقى، كنز العمال، ج8، ص658؛ Tabarī, *Zakhā'ir ol-Oqbā* طبرى، ذخائر العقبى، ص78.

63 Eben Asāker, *at-Tārīkh al-Madīnaʿ ad-Dameshq* ابن عساكر، تاريخ مدينة دمشق، ج42، ص374.

64 Safdī, *al-Wāfī bi'l-Wafyāt* الصفدى، الوافى بالوفيات، ج21، ص179 – 180؛ Eben Abdol-Barr, *al-Estī'āb* ابن عبد البر، الاستيعاب، ج3، ص1108؛ المغربى، فتح الملك العلى، ص71.

65 Eben Abī'l-Hadīd, Abdol-Hamīd, *Sharh-e Nahj ol-Balāgha* ابن أبى الحديد، شرح نهج البلاغة، ج11، ص252 – 255.

66 Tabarī, *al-Ma'jam ol-Kabīr* الطبرانى، المعجم الكبير، ج23، ص329 – 330.

67 Mottaqī al-Hendī, *Kanz ol-A'mmāl* المتقى، كنز العمال، ج11، ص346؛ Eben Asāker, *at-Tārīkh al-Madīnaʿ ad-Dameshq* ابن عساكر، تاريخ مدينة دمشق، ج42، ص459 – 460.

68 Hākem al-Haskānī an-Neyshāpurī, *Shawāhed ot-Tanzīl* الحسكانى، شواهد التنزيل، ج1، ص20.

69 Hākem al-Haskānī an-Neyshāpurī, *Shawāhed ot-Tanzīl* الحسكانى، شواهد التنزيل، ج1، ص20.

70 Hākem al-Haskānī an-Neyshāpurī, *Shawāhed ot-Tanzīl* الحسكانى، شواهد التنزيل، ج1، ص29.

71 Hākem al-Haskānī an-Neyshāpurī, *Shawāhed ot-Tanzīl* الحسكانى، شواهد التنزيل، ج1، ص30.

Endnotes

72 Eben Abdol-Barr, *al-Estī'āb*، ابن عبد البر، الاستيعاب، ج3، ص1104؛ المغربى، فتح الملك العلى، ص71؛ Tabarī، *Zakhā'ir ol-Oqbā* الطبرى، ذخائر العقبى، ص78؛ ابن الدمشقى، جواهر المطالب فى مناقب الإمام على (ع)، ج1، ص194.

73 Al-Barī البرى، الجوهرة فى نسب الإمام على و آله، ص 95.

74 Eben Abī'l-Hadīd, Abdol-Hamīd, *Sharh-e Nahj ol-Balāgha* ابن أبى الحديد، شرح نهج البلاغة، ج1، ص19.

75 Heythamī, *Majma' oz-Zawāed* الهيثمى، مجمع الزوائد، ج9، ص159؛ الطبرى، ذخائر العقبى، ص78.

76 Hākem al-Haskānī an-Neyshāpurī, *Shawāhed ot-Tanzīl* الحسكانى، شواهد التنزيل، ج1، ص39.

77 The leader of a faction of the Khārejites, one of whose members, Eben Moljam, was to kill Imam Ali ﷺ while he was prostrated in the prayer niche of the congregational mosque of Kūfa while leading the evening devotions.

78 Hākem al-Haskānī an-Neyshāpurī, *Shawāhed ot-Tanzīl* الحسكانى، شواهد التنزيل، ج1، ص30.

79 Eben Asāker, *at-Tārīkh al-Madīnať ad-Dameshq* ابن عساكر، تاريخ مدينة دمشق، ج42، ص373.

80 *Ibid.*

81 . المغربى، فتح الملك العلى، ص78.

82 Eben Asāker, *at-Tārīkh al-Madīnať ad-Dameshq* ابن عساكر، تاريخ مدينة دمشق، ج42، ص520؛ Eben Abdol-Barr, *al-Estī'āb* ابن عبد البر، الاستيعاب، ج3، ص 1225؛ Mottaqī al-Hendī, *Kanz ol-A'mmāl* المتقى، كنز العمال، ج13، ص111؛ Balādhurī, *Ansāb ol-Ashrāf* البلاذرى، انساب الأشراف، ص152؛ Eben Kathīr, *al-Badāya wa'l-Nahāya* ابن كثير البداية و النهاية، ج8، ص9.

83 . Eben Abī'l-Hadīd, Abdol-Hamīd, *Sharh-e Nahj ol-Balāgha* ابن أبى الحديد، شرح نهج البلاغة، ج1، ص21.

84 . الحسكانى، شواهد التنزيل، ج1، ص24.

85 . Eben Abī'l-Hadīd, Abdol-Hamīd, *Sharh-e Nahj ol-Balāgha* ابن أبى الحديد، شرح نهج البلاغة، ج4، ص96.

⁸⁶ Eben Abdol-Barr, *al-Estī'āb*, ابن عبد البر، الاستيعاب، ج3، ص1110؛ Eben Abī'l-Hadīd, Abdol-Hamīd, *Sharh-e Nahj ol-Balāgha*, بن أبى الحديد، شرح نهج البلاغة، ج4، ص 95 – 96؛ المغربى، فتح الملك العلى، ص78؛ Eben Athīr, *Osod ol-Ghāba*, ابن الأثير، أسد الغابة، ج4، ص22.

⁸⁷ Eben Abdol-Barr, *al-Estī'āb* ابن عبد البر، الاستيعاب، ج3، ص1104؛ Hākem al-Haskānī an-Neyshāpurī, *Shawāhed ot-Tanzīl* الحسكانى، شواهد التنزيل، ج1، ص49؛ Tabarī, *Zakhā'ir ol-Oqbā*الطبرى، ذخائر العقبى، ص78.

⁸⁸ Ar-Rahmānī, *al-Imām Ali b. Abī-Tāleb* الرحمانى، الإمام على بن أبى طالب (ع)، ص134.

⁸⁹ A pejorative term used for the Shī'a meaning something like a naysayer or one who is a "rejectionist".

⁹⁰ az-Zarandi, *Doror os-Samtayn*, الزرندى، نظم درر السمطين، ص110 – 111.

⁹¹ Eben Nadīm, *Fehrest*. ابن النديم، فهرست ابن النديم، ص111.

⁹² Eben Asāker, *at-Tārīkh al-Madīna' ad-Dameshq* ابن عساكر، تاريخ مدينة دمشق، ج42، ص419.

⁹³ Khatīb al-Baghdādī, *Tarīkh al-Baghdād* البغدادى، تاريخ بغداد، ج1، ص145؛ Eben Asāker, *at-Tārīkh al-Madīna' ad-Dameshq* ابن عساكر، تاريخ مدينة دمشق، ج42، ص446.

⁹⁴ Amīnī, *al-Ghadīr* الأمينى، الغدير، ج10، ص17.

⁹⁵ Ar-Rahmānī, *al-Imām Ali b. Abī-Tāleb* الرحمانى، الإمام على بن أبى طالب (ع)، ص134.

⁹⁶ . أبو الفرج، مقاتل الطالبيين، ص16.

⁹⁷ Manāwī, *Fayḍ ol-Ghadīr* المناوى، فيض القدير، ج4، ص468 – 469.

⁹⁸ . الريشهرى، موسوعة الإمام على بن أبى طالب (ع)، ج8، ص 405 – 407 به نقل ازرساله معراج نامه نوشته ابن سينا.

⁹⁹ Allusion to and condemnation of the illegitimacy of the civil war Mo'āwiya started, stating that he was more deserving of the office.

¹⁰⁰ Eben Asāker, *at-Tārīkh al-Madīna' ad-Dameshq* ابن عساكر، تاريخ مدينة دمشق، ج42، ص419.

¹⁰¹ Rāzī, Fakhroddīn, *Mafātīh ol-Ghayb* الرازى، مفاتيح الغيب، ج1، ص204 – 205.

¹⁰² I.e. those who have a written revelation, usually but not always restricted to Christians and Jews. This category is sometimes extended to Zoroastrians on account of the Avesta and to Hindus on account of the four Vedas, and the Upanisads, the Smrutis, the Puranas, the Ramayana and the Mahabharata (which includes the Bhagavad Gita).

103. Eben Abī'l-Hadīd, Abdol-Hamīd, *Sharh-e Nahj ol-Balāgha*, شرح نهج البلاغة، ج1، ص16 – 30.

104. المرعشى، شرح احقاق الحق، ج30، ص553 به نقل از «على إمام المتقين» (طبع مكتبة غريب الفجالة) نوشته عبد الرحمن الشرقاوى، ج1، ص 29.

105. Another name for Muhammad, meaning the most praised.

106. الآلوسى، روح المعانى، ج29، ص158.

107. Abdoh, *Nahj ol-Balāgha*, عبده، نهج البلاغة، ج1، ص6.

108. Ar-Rahmānī, *al-Imām Ali b. Abī-Tāleb*, الرحمانى، الإمام على بن أبى طالب (ع)، ص140.

109. Ar-Rahmānī, *al-Imām Ali b. Abī-Tāleb* لرحمانى، الإمام على بن أبى طالب (ع)، ص138.

110. المرعشى، شرح احقاق الحق، ج30، ص521 به نقل از «العبقريات الاسلامية» (طبع دار الكتاب اللبنانى، بيروت)، نوشته عباس محمود عقاد ج2، ص 35.

111. حسين، المجموعة الكاملة، ج4، ص443.

112. حسين، المجموعة الكاملة، ج4، ص444.

113. حسن، تاريخ الاسلام، ج1، ص272.

114. المرعشى، شرح احقاق الحق، ج32، ص306 به نقل از «الإمام على بن أبى طالب كرم الله وجهه رابع الخلفاء الراشدين» (طبع دار الكتب العلمية، بيروت) نوشته محمد رضا ص22.

115. *Imam Ali, the voice of Human Justice*, in five volumes; *Ali and Human Rights; Ali and the French Revolution; Ali and Socrates; Ali and His Time; Ali and the Arabs;* and *Masterpieces of the Nahj ol-Balāgha*.

116. Sobhani, quoting George Jordaq السبحانى، لأئمة الإثنى عشر، ص19 به نقل از الإمام على صوت العدالة الإنسانية نوشته جرج جرداق، ج1، ص49.

117. الزركلى، الأعلام، ج4، ص296.

118. Ahmad b. Hanbal, *Masnad* احمد بن حنبل، المسند، ج3، ص3، 62، 64، 82، 391. Eben Māja, *Sonan* ابن ماجه، السنن، ج1، ص44؛ Termedhī, *Sonan* الترمذى، السنن، ج5 ص321.

119. الزرندى، نظم درر السمطين، ص202.

120. Heythamī, *Majma' oz-Zawāed* الهيثمى، مجمع الزوائد، ج9، ص177.

121. Eben Asāker, *at-Tārīkh al-Madīna' ad-Dameshq* ابن عساكر، تاريخ مدينة دمشق، ج13، ص252؛ المزى، تهذيب الكمال، ج6، ص 235 Eben Hajar, *Tahdhīb ot-Tahdhīb* ابن حجر، تهذيب التهذيب، ج2، ص 259؛ Eben Kathīr, *al-Badāya wa'l-Nahāya* ابن كثير، البداية و النهاية، ج8، ص43؛ Eben Borhān ash-Shāfe'ī, *as-Sīra' al-Halabīa* الحلبى، السيرة الحلبية، ج3 ص360.

122. Heythamī, *Majma' oz-Zawā* الهيثمى، مجمع الزوائد، ج9، ص175.

123 Eben Asāker, *at-Tārīkh al-Madīna' ad-Dameshq* ابن عساكر، تاريخ مدينة دمشق، ج13، ص240؛ al-Mezzi, *Tahdhīb al-Kamāl fī Asmā' ar-Rejāl* . تهذيب الكمال، ج6، ص234؛Safdī الصفدى، الوافى بالوفيات، ج12، ص67.

124 Bokhārī, *Sahīh* البخاري، صحيح البخاري، ج4، ص217؛ Eben Hajar al-Asqalānī, *Fath ol-Bārī* ابن حجر، فتح الباري، ج7، ص75؛ العينى، عمدة القاري، ج16، ص242؛ ابن حجر، تغليق التعليق، ج4، ص74؛ Tabarī, Mohebbeddīn, *Dhakhāer ol-Oqbā* الطبرى، ذخائر العقبى، ص127.

125 . المزي، تهذيب الكمال، ج6، ص235.

126 Eben Abdol-Barr, *al-Estī'āb* ابن عبد البر، الاستيعاب، ج1، ص385؛ الكحلانى، سبل السلام، ج1، ص186.

127 Eben Asāker, *at-Tārīkh al-Madīna' ad-Dameshq* ابن عساكر، تاريخ مدينة دمشق، ج13، ص163؛ المزي، تهذيب الكمال، ج6، ص220؛ Eben Hajar, *Tahdhīb ot-Tahdhīb* ابن حجر، تهذيب التهذيب، ج2 ص257.

128 Dhahabī, *Tārīkh al-Islam* الذهبى، تاريخ الإسلام، ج4، ص36.

129 Dhahabī, *Seyr E'lām ol-Anbīyā* الذهبى، سير أعلام النبلاء، ج3، ص 245 – 246.

130 Dhahabī, *Seyr E'lām ol-Anbīyā* الذهبى، سير أعلام النبلاء، ج3، ص253.

131 Safdī, *al-Wāfī bi'l-Wafyāt* الصفدى، الوافى بالوفيات، ج12، ص68.

132 Eben Kathīr, *al-Badāya wa'l-Nahāya* ابن كثير، البداية والنهاية، ج8، ص17.

133 Eben Sabbāq al-Mālekī, *al-Fosūl al-Mohemma* ابن الصباغ، الفصول المهمة، ص156 – 160.

134 . حسين، المجموعة الكاملة، ج4، ص619.

135 . الزركلى، الأعلام، ج2 ص 199.

136 . رضا، الحسن و الحسين سبطا رسول الله، ص14.

137 A contemporary researcher has attempted to gather all of the books written about Imam Hosayn ﷺ in the Arabic and Persian languages by both Shī'a and Sunni authors. He reports 1,428 titles. See Heshmatollāh Safar-Alipour, *Ketābshenāsī-e Ekhtesāsī-e Imām Hosayn* ﷺ.

138 . مراجعه شود به: «ادب الطفّ»، «دانشنامه شعر عاشورائى» و «دانشنامه امام حسين عليه السلام»، ج10، ص185.

139 Dhahabī, *Seyr E'lām ol-Anbīyā* الذهبى، سير أعلام النبلاء، ج3، ص285؛ Eben Hajar ابن حجر، الإصابة، ج2 ص 69؛ Eben Kathīr, *al-Badāya wa'l-Nahāya* ابن كثير، البداية و النهاية، ج8، ص226؛ ابن حجر، تهذيب التهذيب، ج2 ص300؛ الرامهرمزى، الحد الفاصل، ص348؛ الكوفى، المصنف، ج7، ص269؛ Eben Asāker, *at-Tārīkh al-Madīna' ad-Dameshq* ابن عساكر، تاريخ مدينة دمشق، ج14، ص179.

Endnotes

140 Eben Hajar ابن حجر، الإصابة، ج2، ص69؛ Eben Hajar, *Tahdhīb ot-Tahdhīb*، تهذيب التهذيب، ج2، ص300؛ Heythamī الهيثمى، مجمع الزوائد، ج9، ص186؛ الطبرانى، المعجم الأوسط، ج4، ص180؛ المتقى، كنز العمال، ج11، ص343؛ Eben Asāker, *at-Tārīkh al-Madīnaᵗ ad-Dameshq* ابن عساكر، تاريخ مدينة دمشق، ج31، ص275؛ ابن الأثير، أسد الغابة، ج3، ص234.

141 Tabarānī الطبرانى، المعجم الأوسط، ج4، ص181؛ Mottaqī al-Hendī المتقى، كنز العمال، ج11، ص343؛ Eben Kathīr ابن الأثير، أسد الغابة، ج3، ص235؛ *Kanz ol-A'mmāl* القندوزى، ينابيع المودة، ج2، ص43؛ Eben Asāker, *at-Tārīkh al-Madīnaᵗ ad-Dameshq* ابن عساكر، تاريخ مدينة دمشق، ج14، ص276.

142 Eben Asāker, *at-Tārīkh al-Madīnaᵗ ad-Dameshq* ابن عساكر، تاريخ مدينة دمشق، ج14، ص180؛ Dhahabī, *Tārīkh al-Islam* الذهبى، تاريخ الإسلام، ج5، ص102؛ الصفدى، الوافى بالوفيات، ج12، ص263.

143 Dhahabī, *Seyr E'lām ol-Anbīyā* الذهبى، سير أعلام النبلاء، ج3، ص282؛ ا ابن كثير، البداية و النهاية، ج8، ص225.

144 Dhahabī, *Seyr E'lām ol-Anbīyā* الذهبى، سير أعلام النبلاء، ج3، ص280.

145 Eben Sabbāq al-Mālekī, *al-Fosūl al-Mohemma* ابن الصباغ، الفصول المهمّة، ص 174.

146. العقاد، ابو الشهداء الحسين بن على، ص96 ـ 102.

147. المرعشى، شرح احقاق الحق، ج27، ص508، به نقل از «تجديد فى المسلمين لا فى الاسلام» (طبع دار الكتاب العربى، بيروت) نوشته دكتر عمر فروخ، ص152.

148. المرعشى، شرح احقاق الحق، ج27، ص510 به نقل از «أحسن القصص» طبع دار الكتب العلمية، بيروت) نوشته على بن محمد بن عبد الله الفكرى الحسينى القاهرى (م1372ق)، ج4، ص261.

149 Ali Ridā على رضا، غصن الرسول الحسين بن على، ص9.

150 Ali Ridā على رضا، غصن الرسول الحسين بن على، ص305.

151 Ridā رضا، الحسن و الحسين سبطا رسول الله، ص68.

152. الدجانى، الحسين بن على ارادةً و محبةً و جهاد، ص70

153 Bārā بارا، الحسين فى الفكر المسيحى، ص358.

154 Bārā بارا، الحسين فى الفكر المسيحى، ص361.

155 Bārā بارا، الحسين فى الفكر المسيحى، ص363.

156 Bārā بارا، الحسين فى الفكر المسيحى، ص363.

157 Shalbī شلبى، حياة الامام الحسين، ص251.

158 Sharqāwi الشرقاوى، الحسين ثائراً شهيداً، ص13.

159 Eben Asāker, *at-Tārīkh al-Madīnaᵗ ad-Dameshq* ابن عساكر، تاريخ مدينة دمشق، ج41، ص376؛ al-Mezzi, *Tahdhīb al-Kamāl fī Asmā' ar-Rejāl* المزى، تهذيب الكمال، ج20، ص389؛

160. Mar'ashī an-Najafī, *Sharh Ahqāq ol-Haqq*, المرعشى، شرح احقاق الحق، ج12، ص136 به نقل از «محاضرات الأدباء»، (طبع مكتبة الحياة، بيروت)، نوشته راغب اصفهانى، ج 1، ص 344 ؛ ج 4 ص 479.

161. Zereklī, *al-E'lām*. الزركلى، الأعلام، ج7، ص97.

162. Eben Sabbāq al-Mālekī, *al-Fosūl al-Mohemma*; ابن الصباغ، الفصول المهمة، ص203؛ al-Mezzi, *Tahdhīb al-Kamāl fī Asmā' ar-Rejāl* المزى، تهذيب الكمال، ج20، ص386؛ الباجى، التعديل و التجريح، ج 3، ص1078.

163. Eben Asāker, *at-Tārīkh al-Madīna' ad-Dameshq* ابن عساكر، تاريخ مدينة دمشق، ج41، ص366؛ al-Mezzi, *Tahdhīb al-Kamāl fī Asmā' ar-Rejāl* المزى، تهذيب الكمال، ج20، ص384؛ المناوى، فيض القدير، ج1، ص246؛ المباركفورى، تحفة الأحوذى، ج6، ص501؛ Dhahabī, *Seyr E'lām ol-Anbīyā* الذهبى، سير اعلام النبلاء، ج4، ص388.

164. Eben Asāker, *at-Tārīkh al-Madīna' ad-Dameshq* ابن عساكر، تاريخ مدينة دمشق، ج41، ص371؛ al-Mezzi, *Tahdhīb al-Kamāl fī Asmā' ar-Rejāl* المزى، تهذيب الكمال، ج20، ص386؛ Dhahabī, *Tārīkh al-Hoffāz* الذهبى، تذكرة الحفاظ، ج1، ص75. *Seyr* Dhahabī, E'lām ol-Anbīyā الذهبى، سير اعلام النبلاء، ج4، ص389؛ Eben Kathīr, *al-Badāya wa'l-Nahāya* ابن كثير، البداية و النهاية، ج9، ص104؛ ابن العماد، شذرات الذهب، ج1، ص375؛ الباجى، التعديل و التجريح، ج 3، ص1078.

165. Eben-Sa'd, *at-Tabaqāt al-Kobrā*. ابن سعد، الطبقات الكبرى، ج5 ص215؛ Eben Asāker, *at-Tārīkh al-Madīna' ad-Dameshq* ابن عساكر، تاريخ مدينة دمشق، ج41، ص371؛ al-Mezzi, *Tahdhīb al-Kamāl fī Asmā' ar-Rejāl* المزى، تهذيب الكمال، ج20، ص386؛ Dhahabī, *Tārīkh al-Hoffāz* الذهبى، تذكرة الحفاظ، ج1، ص75؛ Eben Kathīr, *al-Badāya wa'l-Nahāya* ابن كثير، البداية و النهاية، ج9، ص104.

166. Eben-Sa'd, *at-Tabaqāt al-Kobrā*, ابن سعد، الطبقات الكبرى، ج5 ص214؛ Eben Kathīr, *al-Badāya wa'l-Nahāya* ابن كثير، البداية و النهاية، ج9، ص108.

167. Eben Asāker, *at-Tārīkh al-Madīna' ad-Dameshq* ابن عساكر، تاريخ مدينة دمشق، ج41، ص373.

168. Eben Asāker, *at-Tārīkh al-Madīna' ad-Dameshq* ابن عساكر، تاريخ مدينة دمشق، ج41، ص373؛ al-Mezzi, *Tahdhīb al-Kamāl fī Asmā' ar-Rejāl* المزى، تهذيب الكمال، ج20، ص387؛ Dhahabī, *Tārīkh al-Hoffāz* الذهبى، تذكرة الحفاظ، ج1، ص75. *Seyr* Dhahabī,

Eben Kathīr, *al-Badāya wa'l-* الذهبى، سير اعلام النبلاء، ج4 ص394؛ *E'lām ol-Anbīyā Nahāya* ابن كثير، البداية و النهاية، ج9، ص104؛ ابن العماد، شذرات الذهب، ج1، ص375. Eben-Sa'd, *at-Tabaqāt al-Kobrā*[169] ابن سعد، الطبقات الكبرى، ج5، ص214؛ Eben Asāker, *at-Tārīkh al-Madīna' ad-Dameshq* ابن عساكر، تاريخ مدينة دمشق، ج41، ص374؛ al-Mezzi, *Tahdhīb al-Kamāl fī Asmā' ar-Rejāl* المزى، تهذيب الكمال، ج20، ص387. Eben Kathīr, *al-Badāya wa'l-Nahāya* ابن كثير، البداية و النهاية، ج9، ص104.

[170] Āyatollāh Mar'ashī relates from twenty different Sunni sources that Imam Zeynol-Ābedīn's ﷺ use to make one thousand cycles of the ritual devotions a day. See Mar'ashī an-Najafī, المرعشى، شرح احقاق الحق، ج12، ص18 ـ 23. *Sharh Ahqāq ol-Haqq*

[171] Eben Asāker, *at-Tārīkh al-Madīna' ad-Dameshq* ابن عساكر، تاريخ مدينة دمشق، ج41، ص378؛ al-Mezzi, *Tahdhīb al-Kamāl fī Asmā' ar-Rejāl* المزى، تهذيب الكمال، ج20، ص390؛ Dhahabī, *Tārīkh al-Hoffāz* الذهبى، تذكرة الحفاظ، ج1، ص75. Dhahabī, *Seyr E'lām ol-Anbīyā* الذهبى، سير اعلام النبلاء، ج4، ص392؛ ابن العماد، شذرات الذهب، ج1، ص376.

[172] al-Mezzi, *Tahdhīb al-Kamāl fī Asmā' ar-Rejāl* المزى، تهذيب الكمال، ج20، ص387؛ Dhahabī, *Seyr E'lām ol-Anbīyā* الذهبى، سير اعلام النبلاء، ج4، ص389؛ Eben Kathīr, *al-Badāya wa'l-Nahāya* ابن كثير، البداية و النهاية، ج9، ص104.

[173] Eben Abī'l-Hadīd, Abdol-Hamīd, *Sharh-e Nahj ol-Balāgha* ابن ابى الحديد، شرح نهج البلاغة، ج15، ص274.

[174] Eben Kathīr, *al-Badāya wa'l-Nahāya* ابن كثير، البداية و النهاية، ج9، ص122.

[175] Eben-Sa'd, *at-Tabaqāt al-Kobrā* ابن سعد، الطبقات الكبرى، ج5، ص222؛ Eben Asāker, *at-Tārīkh al-Madīna' ad-Dameshq* ابن عساكر، تاريخ مدينة دمشق، ج41، ص362.

[176] Mar'ashī an-Najafī, *Sharh Ahqāq ol-Haqq* المرعشى، شرح احقاق الحق، ج12، ص12 به نقل از «الفاضل» (طبع دارالكتب، مصر)، نوشته المبرد، ص103.

[177] Eben Asāker, *at-Tārīkh al-Madīna' ad-Dameshq* ابن عساكر، تاريخ مدينة دمشق، ج41، ص374؛ al-Mezzi, *Tahdhīb al-Kamāl fī Asmā' ar-Rejāl* المزى، تهذيب الكمال، ج20، ص388. Dhahabī, *Seyr E'lām ol-Anbīyā* الذهبى، سير اعلام النبلاء، ج4، ص390.

[178] Ya'qūbī, *at-Tārīkh* اليعقوبى، تاريخ اليعقوبى، ج2، ص303.

[179] ابن حبان، مشاهير علماء الامصار، ص104.

[180] Mar'ashī an-Najafī, *Sharh Ahqāq ol-Haqq* المرعشى، شرح احقاق الحق، ج12، ص129 به نقل از «حلية الاولياء» (طبع مطبعة السعاة، مصر)، نوشته ابونعيم اصفهانى، ج3، ص133.

¹⁸¹ *Motewāter* – A technical term which makes its appearance in the science of *hadīth*, referring to a report that has been transmitted by so many different transmitters (and in different chains of custody) with the exact same wording so as not to leave room for a shadow of a doubt as to the integrity both as to the chain of custody and as to the reliability of the text itself.

¹⁸² Eben Abi'l-Hadīd, Abdol-Hamīd, *Sharh-e Nahj ol-Balāgha* ابن ابى الحديد، شرح نهج البلاغة، ج15، ص277.

¹⁸³ Mar'ashī an-Najafī, *Sharh Ahqāq ol-Haqq* المرعشى، شرح احقاق الحق، ج28، ص7، به نقل از «أحسن القصص» (طبع دارالكتب العلمية، بيروت)، نوشته على فكرى الحسينى المصرى، ج4، ص265.

¹⁸⁴ Ya'qūbī, *at-Tārīkh* الذهبى، سير اعلام النبلاء، ج4، ص398.

¹⁸⁵ Eben Kathīr, *Tafsīr al-Quran al-Azīm* ابن كثير، تفسير القرآن العظيم، ج2، ص591.

¹⁸⁶ Mar'ashī an-Najafī, *Sharh Ahqāq ol-Haqq*, quoting Ahmad b. Hanbal المرعشى، شرح احقاق الحق، ج12، ص130 به نقل از «الصارم المنكى فى الرد على السبكى» (طبع مطبعة الإمام)، نوشته محمد بن أحمد بن عبد الهادى حنبلى، ص 99..

¹⁸⁷ See footnote 180.

¹⁸⁸ Eben Sabbāq al-Mālekī, *al-Fosūl al-Mohemma* ابن الصباغ، الفصول المهمة، ص200.

¹⁸⁹ Qondūzī, *Yanabī al-Mawadda* القندوزى، ينابيع المودة، ص378.

¹⁹⁰ Mar'ashī an-Najafī, *Sharh Ahqāq ol-Haqq* المرعشى، شرح احقاق الحق، ج28، ص6، به نقل از «تعليقة فتح الباقى على ألفية العراقى» (طبع دار الكتب العلمية بيروت)، نوشته زكريا بن محمد بن أحمد بن زكريا الأنصارى السنكى، ج1، ص24.

¹⁹¹ ابن طولون، الائمة الاثنا عشر، ص78.

¹⁹² Eben Hajar, *as-Sawā'eq ol-Mahraqa* ابن حجر الهيتمى، الصواعق المحرقة، ص201.

¹⁹³ الشوكانى، نيل الاوطار، ج1، ص23.

¹⁹⁴ Qondūzī, *Yanabī al-Mawadda* القندوزى، ينابيع المودة، ص153.

¹⁹⁵ المباركفورى، تحفة الأحوذى، ج6، ص501.

¹⁹⁶ Mar'ashī an-Najafī, *Sharh Ahqāq ol-Haqq* المرعشى، شرح احقاق الحق، ج12، ص135 به نقل از «الروضة الندية»، (طبع الخيرية، مصر)، نوشته مصطفى رشدى، ص12.

¹⁹⁷ الآلوسى، تفسير الآلوسى، ج3 ص356.

¹⁹⁸ Zereklī, *al- E'lām* الزركلى، الأعلام، ج4، ص 277.

¹⁹⁹ Mar'ashī an-Najafī, *Sharh Ahqāq ol-Haqq* المرعشى، شرح احقاق الحق، ج28، ص110. به نقل از «إحداث التاريخ الإسلامى بترتيب السنين» (طبع كويت)، نوشته دكتر عبدالسلام الترمانينى، ج1، ص632.

²⁰⁰ Mar'ashī an-Najafī, *Sharh Ahqāq ol-Haqq* المرعشى، شرح احقاق الحق، ج28، ص146. به نقل از «أئمة الفقه التسعة»، (طبع الهيئة المصرية العامة للكتاب)، نوشته عبد الرحمن شرقاوى، ج1، ص23.

Endnotes

201 Mar'ashī an-Najafī, *Sharh Ahqāq ol-Haqq*, المرعشي، شرح احقاق الحق، ج 28، ص192، به نقل از «الإمام جعفر الصادق»، (طبع المجلس الأعلى للشئون الإسلامية، القاهرة)، نوشته عبد الحليم الجندي، ص 134.

202 Mar'ashī an-Najafī, *Sharh Ahqāq ol-Haqq*, المرعشي، شرح احقاق الحق، ج 28، ص152، به نقل از «العلم والعلماء» (طبع دار الكتب السلفية)، نوشته جابر الجزائري، ص 25.

203 Mar'ashī an-Najafī, *Sharh Ahqāq ol-Haqq*, المرعشي، شرح احقاق الحق، ج28، ص192، به نقل از «آل بيت النبي في مصر» (طبع دارالمعارف، القاهرة)، نوشته احمد ابوكف، ص 59.

204 Mar'ashī an-Najafī, *Sharh Ahqāq ol-Haqq*, المرعشي، شرح احقاق الحق، ج28، ص 30، به نقل از «تراجم الرجال» (طبع التعاونية)، نوشته محمد الخضر حسين، ص 25.

205 Mar'ashī an-Najafī, *Sharh Ahqāq ol-Haqq* 205 المرعشي، شرح احقاق الحق، ج19، ص439، به نقل از «الأنوار القدسية» (طبع السعادة مصر)، نوشته ياسين بن إبراهيم السنهوتي الشافعي، ص 33.

206 Ya'qūbī, *at-Tārīkh*;320 ص، 2ج، تاريخ اليعقوبي، اليعقوبي، Eben Kathīr, *al-Badāya wa'l-Nahāya*; 339 ص، 9ج، البداية و النهاية، ابن كثير، Eben Khallakān, *Wafyāt al-'Ayān* ابن خلكان،وفيات الاعيان، ج4، ص 174؛ القرطبي، تفسير القرطبي، ج1، ص445؛ Nawawi شرح صحيح مسلم، ج1، ص103؛ القاري، شرح مسند ابي حنيفة، ص211. الجوهري، الصحاح، ج2، ص 595؛ ابن منظور، لسان العرب، ج4، ص74؛ الفيروزآبادي، القاموس المحيط، ج1، ص376. آيت الله مرعشي نجفي در اين باره از بيست منبع اهل سنت نقل سخن كرده است، مراجعه شود به: المرعشي، شرح احقاق الحق، ج12، ص160 ـ 165. See Mar'ashī an-Najafī, *Sharh Ahqāq ol-Haqq*

207 Eben Hajar, *Tahdhīb ot-Tahdhīb* ابن حجر، تهذيب التهذيب، ج9، ص313.

208 Eben Asāker, *at-Tārīkh al-Madīnaʻ ad-Dameshq* ابن عساكر، تاريخ مدينة دمشق، ج54، ص278؛ ابن كثير، البداية و النهاية، ج9، ص340.

209 Eben-Sa'd, *at-Tabaqāt al-Kobrā* ابن سعد، الطبقات الكبرى، ج5، ص 324؛ Eben Asāker, *at-Tārīkh al-Madīnaʻ ad-Dameshq* ابن كثير، تاريخ مدينة دمشق، ج54، ص276.

210 . محمد بن طلحه، مطالب السؤول، ص 425.

211 Eben Abī'l-Hadīd, Abdol-Hamīd, *Sharh-e Nahj ol-Balāgha* ابن ابى الحديد، شرح نهج البلاغة، ج15، ص 277.

212 Nawawi. النووي، شرح صحيح مسلم، ج6، ص 137.

213 Eben Khallakān, *Wafyāt al-'Ayān*. ابن خلكان، وفيات الاعيان، ج4، ص174.

214 . الذهبي، سير اعلام النبلاء، ج4، ص401.

215 Dhahabī, *Tārīkh al-Hoffāz* الذهبي، تذكرة الحفاظ، ج1، ص 124.

216 Eben Kathīr, *al-Badāya wa'l-Nahāya* ابن كثير، البداية و النهاية، ج9، ص 338.

217 . ابن طولون، الائمة الاثنا عشر، ص 81.

218 Eben Hajar, *as-Sawā'eq ol-Mahraqa* ابن حجر الهيتمي، الصواعق المحرقة، ص 201.

219. الزبیدی، تاج العروس، ج3، ص55.

220. المرعشی Mar'ashī an-Najafī, *Sharh Ahqāq ol-Haqq*، شرح احقاق الحق، ج12، ص170 به نقل از «الروضة الندیة» (طبع الخیریة، مصر)، نوشته مصطفی رشدی، ص12.

221. المناوی، فیض القدیر، ج1، ص15.

222. المرعشی Mar'ashī an-Najafī, *Sharh Ahqāq ol-Haqq*، شرح احقاق الحق، ج12، ص181 به نقل از «جامع کرامات الاولیاء» (طبع مصطفی الحلبی، قاهره)، نوشته یوسف بن اسماعیل نبهانی ج1، ص164..

223. المرعشی Mar'ashī an-Najafī, *Sharh Ahqāq ol-Haqq*، شرح احقاق الحق، ج28، ص292 به نقل از «أحسن القصص» (طبع دار الکتب العلمیة، بیروت)، نوشته علی بن الدکتور محمد عبد الله فکری الحسینی، ج4، ص276.

224. المرعشی Mar'ashī an-Najafī, *Sharh Ahqāq ol-Haqq*، شرح احقاق الحق، ج19، ص489 به نقل از «الأنوار القدسیة» (طبع السعادة بمصر)، نوشته یاسین بن إبراهیم السنهوتی الشافعی، ص34.

225. المرعشی Mar'ashī an-Najafī, *Sharh Ahqāq ol-Haqq*، شرح احقاق الحق، ج28، ص293 به نقل از «تراجم الرجال» (طبع المطبعة التعاونیة)، نوشته محمد الخضر حسین، ص29.

226. Eben Abdol-Barr, *al-Tamhīd* ابن عبد البر، التمهید، ج2، ص66.

227. Eben Abī'l-Hadīd, Abdol-Hamīd, *Sharh-e Nahj ol-Balāgha* ابن ابی الحدید، شرح نهج البلاغة، ج1، ص18.

228. ابن عدی، الکامل، ج2، ص132؛ الذهبی، تاریخ الإسلام، ج9، ص88؛ المناوی، فیض القدیر، ج2، ص255؛ المزی، تهذیب الکمال، ج5، ص74؛ الصفدی، الوافی بالوفیات، ج9، ص98؛ الذهبی، سیر أعلام النبلاء، ج6، ص258.

229. ابن حبان، الثقات، ج6، ص131.

230. النیشابوری، معرفة علوم الحدیث، ص55.

231. Eben Abdol-Barr, *al-Tamhīd* ابن عبد البر، التمهید، ج2، ص66.

232. المرعشی Mar'ashī an-Najafī, *Sharh Ahqāq ol-Haqq*، شرح احقاق الحق، ج33، ص 807، به نقل از «المنتظم فی تاریخ الملوک والأمم» (دار الکتب العلمیة بیروت) نوشته أبو الفرج عبد الرحمن بن علی بن محمد ابن الجوزی، ج8، ص110.

233. محمد بن طلحه، مطالب السؤول، ص436.

234. Eben Abī'l-Hadīd, Abdol-Hamīd, *Sharh-e Nahj ol-Balāgha* ابن ابی الحدید، شرح نهج البلاغة، ج15، ص274.

235 Located in Medīna and wherein the Prophet ﷺ and some of the members of his family are buried.

236. Nawawi. النووی، المجموع، ج8، ص275.

237. Eben Khallakān, *Wafyāt al-'Ayān* ابن خلکان، وفیات الاعیان، ج1، ص327.

238. Dhahabī, *Tārīkh al-Hoffāz*، الذهبی، تذکرة الحفاظ، ج1، ص166.
239. Eben Khallakān, *Wafyāt al-'Ayān* ابن خلکان، الوافی بالوفیات، ج11، ص99.
240. Eben Hajar, *Tahdhīb ot-Tahdhīb* ابن حجر، تقریب التهذیب، ج1، ص163.
241. Eben Sabbāq al-Mālekī, *al-Fosūl al-Mohemma* ابن الصباغ، الفصول المهمة، ج2، ص907.
242. Eben Sabbāq al-Mālekī, *al-Fosūl al-Mohemma* ابن الصباغ، الفصول المهمة، ج2، ص927.
243. ابن طولون، الائمة الاثنا عشر، ص81.
244. Eben Hajar, *as-Sawā'eq ol-Mahraqa* ابن حجر الهیتمی، الصواعق المحرقة، ص201.
245. Mar'ashī an-Najafī, *Sharh Ahqāq ol-Haqq* المرعشی، شرح احقاق الحق، ج33، ص808 به نقل از «جامع کرامات الأولیاء» (طبع مصطفی البابی وشرکاه، مصر)، نوشته یوسف بن إسماعیل النبهانی، ج2، ص4.
246. الآلوسی، تفسیر الآلوسی، ج2، ص395.
247. الآلوسی، تفسیر الآلوسی، ج1، ص82.
248. المبارکفوری، تحفة الأحوذی، ج1، ص115؛ ج3، ص43.
249. جماعة من العلماء، التوفیق الربانی فی الرد علی ابن تیمیة الحرانی، ص196.
250. Zereklī, *al-E'lām* الزرکلی، الاعلام، ج2، ص126؛ Mar'ashī an-Najafī, *Sharh Ahqāq ol-Haqq* المرعشی، شرح احقاق الحق، ج28، ص512، به نقل از «تعلیقه علی کتاب مشارق أنوار العقول» (طبع دار الجیل، بیروت)، نوشته شیخ عبد الله السالمی الأباضی، ج1، ص86.
251. Mar'ashī an-Najafī, *Sharh Ahqāq ol-Haqq* المرعشی، شرح احقاق الحق، ج12، ص214 به نقل از «نزهة الجلیس» (طبع القاهره) نوشته سید عباس مکی، ج2، ص35؛ ج1، ص50.
252. An unheard of number for that era (or in ours, for that matter).
253. Mar'ashī an-Najafī, *Sharh Ahqāq ol-Haqq* المرعشی، شرح احقاق الحق، ج12، ص218 به نقل از «أئمة الهدی» (طبع القاهرة)، نوشته سید محمد بن عبد الغفار الهاشمی الأفغانی، ص117.
254. ابوزهرة، الامام الصادق، 3.
255. Mar'ashī an-Najafī, *Sharh Ahqāq ol-Haqq* المرعشی، شرح احقاق الحق، ج28، ص326. به نقل از «تاریخ المذاهب الاسلامی» (طبع دار الفکر العربی)، نوشته شیخ محمد أبو زهرة، ص713.
256. Mar'ashī an-Najafī, *Sharh Ahqāq ol-Haqq* المرعشی، شرح احقاق الحق، ج28، ص446. به نقل از «المیراث عند الجعفریة»، (طبع دار الرائد العربی، بیروت)، نوشته محمد ابو زهرة، ص34.
257. Mar'ashī an-Najafī, *Sharh Ahqāq ol-Haqq* المرعشی، شرح احقاق الحق، ج12، ص217. به نقل از «مالک حیاته و عصره و آراؤه و فقهه» (طبع مطبعة مخیم، مصر)، نوشته شیخ أبو محمد زهره المصری المالکی، ص104.
258. Mar'ashī an-Najafī, *Sharh Ahqāq ol-Haqq* المرعشی، شرح احقاق الحق، ج19، ص505. به نقل از «الأنوار القدسیة» (طبع السعادة، مصر)، نوشته شیخ إبراهیم بن یاسین السنهوتی الشافعی، ص36.

259 Mar'ashī an-Najafī, *Sharh Ahqāq ol-Haqq*, المرعشى، شرح احقاق الحق، ج19، ص508.
به نقل از «المشرع الروى» (طبع القاهرة) نوشته سيد محمد بن أبى بكر بن عبد الله بن علوى الحضرمى، ص35.

260 Mar'ashī an-Najafī, *Sharh Ahqāq ol-Haqq*, المرعشى، شرح احقاق الحق، ج28، ص315.
به نقل از «سبائك الذهب» (طبع بيروت)، نوشته أبو الفوز محمد بن أمين، ص 329.

261 Mar'ashī an-Najafī, *Sharh Ahqāq ol-Haqq*, المرعشى، شرح احقاق الحق، ج28، ص316.
به نقل از «أحداث التاريخ الاسلامى بترتيب السنين» (طبع الكويت)، نوشته الدكتور عبد السلام الترمانينى، ج2، ص916.

262 Mar'ashī an-Najafī, *Sharh Ahqāq ol-Haqq*, المرعشى، شرح احقاق الحق، ج28، ص317.
به نقل از «معجم العلماء العرب» (طبع عالم الكتب و مكتبة النهضة العربية، بيروت)، نوشته باقر أمين الورد، ج1، ص94.

263 Mar'ashī an-Najafī, *Sharh Ahqāq ol-Haqq*, المرعشى، شرح احقاق الحق، ج28، ص449.
به نقل از «مناهج الشريعة الاسلامية» (طبع مكتبة المعارف، بيروت)، نوشته شيخ أحمد محيى الدين العجوز، ج3، ص114.

264 Mar'ashī an-Najafī, *Sharh Ahqāq ol-Haqq*, المرعشى، شرح احقاق الحق، ج28، ص450.
به نقل از «أئمة الفقه التسعة»، (طبع الهيئة المصرية العامة للكتاب)، نوشته عبد الرحمن الشرقاوى، ج1، ص27.

265 الجندى، الإمام جعفر الصادق، ص63.

266 Mar'ashī an-Najafī, *Sharh Ahqāq ol-Haqq*, المرعشى، شرح احقاق الحق، ج28، ص512.
به نقل از «المدخل إلى دراسة الأديان والمذاهب» (طبع دار العربية للموسوعات)، نوشته عبد الرزاق محمد أسود، ج3 ص82.

267 آل على، الامام الصادق كما عرفه علماء الغرب، ص10.

268 Eben Hajar, *Tahdhīb ot-Tahdhīb*, ابن حجر، تهذيب التهذيب، ج10، ص302؛ ابن حجر، لسان الميزان، ج7، ص402؛ Dhahabī, *Tārīkh al-Islam*, الذهبى، تاريخ الإسلام، ج12، ص417؛ Dhahabī, Seyr E'lām ol-Anbīyā الذهبى، سير أعلام النبلاء، ج6، ص270؛ al-Mezzī, *Tahdhīb al-Kamāl fī Asmā' ar-Rejāl* المزى، تهذيب الكمال، ج29، ص43.

269 Ya'qūbī, *at-Tārīkh* اليعقوبى، تاريخ اليعقوبى، ج2، ص414.

270 Mar'ashī an-Najafī, *Sharh Ahqāq ol-Haqq*, المرعشى، شرح احقاق الحق، ج33، ص 821.
به نقل از «المنتظم فى تاريخ الملوك والأمم» (طبع دار الكتب العلمية، بيروت)، نوشته أبو الفرج عبد الرحمن بن على بن محمد ابن الجوزى، ج9، ص87.

271 *Tawassol* is a specific type of intercessory recourse in which someone resorts to or takes recourse in various instruments that have been made available to him by God ﷻ (such as the supplications or the spirit of a prophet or saint) as an intermediary means for help in his endeavors to recommend himself to the notice and favor or mercy of God ﷻ.

Endnotes

272. محمد بن طلحه، مطالب السؤول، ص447.
273. Eben Jowzī, *Tazkerat ol-Khawās*, ابن الجوزی، تذكرة الخواص، ص348.
274. Eben Abī'l-Hadīd, Abdol-Hamīd, *Sharh-e Nahj ol-Balāgha* ابن ابى الحديد، شرح نهج البلاغة، ج15، ص291.
275. المزى، تهذيب الكمال، ج29، ص44؛ Dhahabī, *Seyr E'lām ol-Anbīyā* الذهبى، سير أعلام النبلاء، ج6، ص271.
276. Dhahabī, *Tārīkh al-Islam* الذهبى، تاريخ الاسلام، ج12، ص417.
277. Mar'ashī an-Najafī, *Sharh Ahqāq ol-Haqq*, المرعشى، شرح احقاق الحق، ج 12، ص301 به نقل از مرآة الجنان (ط حيدر آباد)، نوشته علامه يافعى، ج1، ص394.
278. Eben Kathīr, *al-Badāya wa'l-Nahāya* ابن كثير، البداية و النهاية، ج10، ص197.
279. Eben Sabbāq al-Mālekī, *al-Fosūl al-Mohemma* ابن الصباغ، الفصول المهمة، ج2، ص937.
280. In Islam, charity has its reward with God 🌺, but charity given anonymously has a much greater reward.
281. Eben Sabbāq al-Mālekī, *al-Fosūl al-Mohemm.* ابن الصباغ، الفصول المهمة، ج2، ص949.
282. Qondūzī, *Yanabī al-Mawadda* القندوزى، ينابيع المودة، ص382.
283. See footnote 271.
284. Eben Hajar, *as-Sawā'eq ol-Mahraqa* ابن حجر الهيتمى، الصواعق المحرقة، ص203.
285. See footnote 271.
286. Mar'ashī an-Najafī, *Sharh Ahqāq ol-Haqq*, المرعشى، شرح احقاق الحق، ج12، ص300، به نقل از «إسعاف الراغبين» (طبع شده در هامش نور الابصار طبع العثمانية، مصر)، نوشته محمد بن على الصبان المالكى، ص247.
287. Mar'ashī an-Najafī, *Sharh Ahqāq ol-Haqq*, المرعشى، شرح احقاق الحق، ج33، ص832، به نقل از «جامع كرامات الأولياء» (طبع مصطفى البابى و شركاه، مصر)، نوشته يوسف بن إسماعيل النبهانى، ج2، ص495.
288. See footnote 271.
289. Mar'ashī an-Najafī, *Sharh Ahqāq ol-Haqq*, المرعشى، شرح احقاق الحق، ج12، ص300، به نقل از «الروضة الندية» (طبع الخيرية، مصر)، نوشته شيخ مصطفى رشدى ابن الشيخ إسماعيل الدمشقى، ص11.
290. See footnote 271.
291. Mar'ashī an-Najafī, *Sharh Ahqāq ol-Haqq*, المرعشى، شرح احقاق الحق، ج19، ص358، به نقل از «الأنوار القدسية». (طبع السعادة، مصر)، نوشته شيخ ياسين بن إبراهيم السنهوتى الشافعى، ص38.
292. Zereklī, *al- E'lām* الزركلى، الاعلام، ج7، ص321.

293 المرعشى، شرح احقاق الحق، ج12، ص300. Mar'ashī an-Najafī, *Sharh Ahqāq ol-Haqq*.
به نقل از «الكواكب الدرية»، (طبع الأزهرية، مصر) نوشته شيخ عبد الرؤف المناوى، ج1، ص172.
294 See footnote 270.
295 المرعشى، شرح احقاق الحق، ج28، ص553. Mar'ashī an-Najafī, *Sharh Ahqāq ol-Haqq*.
به نقل از «البصائر لمنكر التوسل بأهل المقابر»، (طبع إسلامبول، سال 1398ق)، نوشته حمد الله الهندى الداجوى الحنفى، ص42.
296 الطبرى، تاريخ الطبرى، ج7، ص139؛ Tabarī, *Tārīkh ar-Rosol wa'l-Molūk*. Dhahabī, *Seyr E'lām ol-Anbīyā* الذهبى، سير أعلام النبلاء، ج9، ص390؛ ابن النجار، ذيل تاريخ بغداد، ج4، ص140.
297 The clan to which the Prophet ﷺ and the Members of his House belong.
298 . ابن حبان، الثقات، ج8، ص456.
299 المرعشى، شرح احقاق الحق، ج28، ص565. Mar'ashī an-Najafī, *Sharh Ahqāq ol-Haqq*.
به نقل از «التبيين فى أنساب القرشيين» (طبع بيروت)، نوشته الموفق أبو محمد عبد الله بن أحمد بن محمد بن قدامة المقدسى، ص133.
300 One who was legendary for his generosity and alms-giving.
301 . محمد بن طلحه، مطالب السؤول، ص455.
302 ابن أبى الحديد، Eben Abī'l-Hadīd, Abdol-Hamīd, *Sharh-e Nahj ol-Balāgha* شرح نهج البلاغة، ج15، ص291.
303 الذهبى، سير أعلام النبلاء، ج9، ص387. Dhahabī, *Seyr E'lām ol-Anbīyā*.
304 الذهبى، تاريخ الإسلام، ج14، ص 270. Dhahabī, *Tārīkh al-Islam*.
305 ابن حجر، تهذيب التهذيب، ج7، ص340؛ السمعانى، الأنساب، Eben Hajar, *Tahdhīb ot-Tahdhīb*. ج3 ص74.
306 المرعشى، شرح احقاق الحق، ج19، ص554. Mar'ashī an-Najafī, *Sharh Ahqāq ol-Haqq*.
به نقل از «الإتحاف بحب الاشراف»، (طبع مصطفى البابى الحلبى، مصر)، نوشته عبد الله بن محمد بن عامر الشبراوى الشافعى، ص58.
307 المرعشى، شرح احقاق الحق، ج12، ص343. Mar'ashī an-Najafī, *Sharh Ahqāq ol-Haqq*.
به نقل از «جامع كرامات الأولياء» (طبع الحبلى، مصر)، نوشته شيخ يوسف بن إسماعيل النبهانى، ج2، ص311.
308 See footnote 279.
309 المرعشى، شرح احقاق الحق، ج28، ص622. Mar'ashī an-Najafī, *Sharh Ahqāq ol-Haqq*.
به نقل از «أحسن القصص»، (طبع دار الكتب العلمية، بيروت)، نوشته على بن الدكتور محمد عبد الله فكرى الحسينى القاهرى، ج4، ص 289.
310 المرعشى، شرح احقاق الحق، ج28، ص597. Mar'ashī an-Najafī, *Sharh Ahqāq ol-Haqq*.
به نقل از «المجددون فى الاسلام»، (طبع مكتبة الآداب ومطبعتها)، نوشته الأستاذ عبد المتعال الصعيدى المصرى، ص88.

³¹¹ Mar'ashī an-Najafī, *Sharh Ahqāq ol-Haqq*, المرعشى، شرح احقاق الحق، ج19، ص554.
به نقل از «الأنوار القدسية»، (طبع السعادة، مصر)، نوشته شيخ ياسين بن إبراهيم السنهوتى الشافعى، ص39.

³¹² . محمد بن طلحه، مطالب السؤول، ص467.

³¹³ Eben Jowzī, *Tazkerat ol-Khawās*. ابن الجوزى، تذكرة الخواص، ص359.

³¹⁴ . الشاكرى، موسوعة المصطفى والعترة عليه السلام، ج13، ص541، به نقل از «منهاج السنة»، نوشته تقى الدين أحمد بن عبد الحليم الشهير بابن تيمية الحرانى الدمشقى الحنبلى.

³¹⁵ . الشاكرى، موسوعة المصطفى والعترة عليه السلام، ج13، ص540، به نقل از «معارج الوصول إلى معرفة فضل آل الرسول والبتول»، نوشته: محمد بن يوسف بن الحسن الأنصارى.

³¹⁶ *Zehār*: this is the most final form of divorce, where the man proclaims his wife to be unlawful unto him "as my mother is unlawful unto me". As such, it does not require a "waiting period" [of three menstrual cycles] during which she cannot be remarried (*'idda*) before the two can marry again, but a marriage can take place again (immediately) if the man repents of his action and pays the atonement price (*kaffāra*).

³¹⁷ A *raj'ī* divorce is a divorce in which the man can 'return' (*raj'a'*) to his (erstwhile "divorced") wife during the wife's waiting period (*'idda*), and continue marital relations without the need for a new marriage contract (*nekāh*).

³¹⁸ In addition to the source quoted (Eben Hajar al-Heythamī's *Sawāeq ol-Marhaqa*, page 206), Āyatollāh al-Mar'ashī an-Najafī has related this report from eleven other Sonnī sources in his *Sharh Ahqāq ol-Haqq* commentary.

³¹⁹ Eben Hajar, *as-Sawā'eq ol-Mahraqa* ابن حجر الهيتمى، الصواعق المحرقة، ص206. آيت الله مرعشى نجفى اين خبر را علاوه بر ابن حجر هيتمى از يازده منبع ديگر از منابع اهل‌سنت نقل كرده است، مراجعه شود به: المرعشى، شرح احقاق الحق، ج12، ص424؛ ج19، ص586؛ ج29، ص9.

³²⁰ Mar'ashī an-Najafī, *Sharh Ahqāq ol-Haqq* المرعشى، شرح احقاق الحق، ج19، ص585.
به نقل از «مفتاح العارف» (مخطوط)، نوشته الخواجة المولوى عبد الفتاح ابن محمد نعمان الحنفى الهندى.

³²¹ Mar'ashī an-Najafī, *Sharh Ahqāq ol-Haqq*, المرعشى، شرح احقاق الحق، ج33، ص874.
به نقل از «جامع كرامات الأولياء»، (طبع مصطفى البابى وشركاه، مصر)، نوشته يوسف بن إسماعيل النبهانى، ج1، ص168.

³²² Mar'ashī an-Najafī, *Sharh Ahqāq ol-Haqq* المرعشى، شرح احقاق الحق، ج29، ص3، به نقل از «أحداث التاريخ الاسلامى بترتيب السنين» (طبع الكويت)، نوشته الدكتور عبد السلام الترمانينى، ج2، ص1259.ت.

³²³ Zereklī, *al-E'lām* الزركلى، الاعلام، ج7، ص155.

[324] Mar'ashī an-Najafī, *Sharh Ahqāq ol-Haqq*, المرعشى، شرح احقاق الحق، ج29، ص15، به نقل از «أحسن القصص»، (طبع بيروت)، نوشته على الحسينى فكرى القاهرى، ج4، ص295.
[325] محمد بن طلحه، مطالب السؤول، ص471.
[326] Eben Kathīr, *al-Badāya wa'l-Nahāya*, ابن كثير، البداية و النهاية، ج11، ص15.
[327] Qondūzī, *Yanabī al-Mawadda*, القندوزى، ينابيع المودة، ص386.
[328] Eben Hajar, *as-Sawā'eq ol-Mahraqa*, ابن حجر الهيتمى، الصواعق المحرقة، ص207.
[329] Mar'ashī an-Najafī, *Sharh Ahqāq ol-Haqq*, المرعشى، شرح احقاق الحق، ج29، ص38، به نقل از «الشذرات»، (طبع دار إحياء التراث العربى، بيروت)، نوشته أبو الفلاح عبد الحى ابن العماد الحنبلى، ج2، ص128.
[330] Zereklī, *al- E'lām*, الزركلى، الاعلام، ج5 ص140.
[331] Mar'ashī an-Najafī, *Sharh Ahqāq ol-Haqq*, المرعشى، شرح احقاق الحق، ج29، ص32، به نقل از «أحسن القصص»، (طبع دار الكتب العلمية، بيروت)، نوشته على بن الدكتور محمد عبد الله فكرى الحسينى القاهرى، ج4، ص300.
[332] Eben Jowzī, *Tazkerat ol-Khawās*, ابن الجوزى، تذكرة الخواص، ص362.
[333] Zereklī, *al- E'lām*, الزركلى، الاعلام، ج2، ص215.

[334] It would seem that what is meant by our esteemed author here is the avoidance of sectarian division which at times has even led to the heresy of excommunication (*takfīr*).

[335] The reference here is to the *Hadīth ath-Thaqalayn* or the Hadīth of the Two Weighty Trusts. It is one of the most widely accepted and authoritative of all the reports narrated from the Prophet ﷺ and it has also been recorded in the principal Sonnī collections of *hadīth*. It possesses the highest degree of authenticity and acceptance, and one of the redactions reads as follows: "I leave among you two precious and weighty trusts, one being the Book of God ﷻ and the other my Family [*etratī*; other redactions have it as my House, *ahl baytī*]. These two legacies will never be separated from each other, and if you lay firm hold of them you will never go astray." (Moslem, *al-Sahih*, Vol. VII, p. 122; at-Termedhī, *Jami' al-Sahih*, Vol. II, p. 308 & 5:328 (hadīth 3874); al-Hākem, *al-Mostadrak*, Vol. III, p. 109 & 533. In his digest of the *Mostadrak*, Dhahabī has deemed this report to be *sahih*, agreeing with al-Hākem. See also, Ahmad b. Hanbal, *al-Masnad*, Vol. III, pp. 14-17 & 5: 181-9; Nesāī's *khasāes* p. 21; and al-Muttaqi, al-Hindi's *kanz ol-a'māl* 1:44, 47-48; Dārami's *sonan* 2:431; Eben Sa'd, *tabaqāt al-kobrā*, 2:2; Ibn al-

Sabbagh, *Fusul al-Muhimmah*, p. 24; al-Ganji, *Kifayat al-Talib*, p. 130; al-Qonduzi, Yanabi' *al-Mawaddah*, pp. 17-18; al-Ya'qubi, *al-Tarikh*, Vol. II, p. 92; Fakhr al-Din al-Razi, *al-Tafsir al-Kabir*, Vol. III, p. 18; al-Naysaburi, *Ghara'ib al-Quran*, Vol. I, p. 349.) Certain Sonnī scholars even add the following sentence at the end of the *hadīth*: "Ali is always with the Quran and the Quran is [always] with Ali; they too will not be separated from each other." (al-Qunduzi, *Yanabi' al-Mawaddah*, pp. 32-40; Ibn Hajar, *al-Sawa'iq*, p. 57; al-Irbidi, *Kashf al-Ghomma'*, p.43.)

NOTES:

www.ingramcontent.com/pod-product-compliance
Lightning Source LLC
Chambersburg PA
CBHW011317080526
44588CB00020B/2734